T0267186

THE WITHDRAWAL

THE WITHDRAWAL

IRAQ, LIBYA, AFGHANISTAN, AND
THE FRAGILITY OF U.S. POWER

NOAM CHOMSKY
AND VIJAY PRASHAD

THE
NEW
PRESS

NEW YORK
LONDON

Requests for permission to reproduce selections from this book should be made
through our website: https://thenewpress.com/contact.

Published in the United States by The New Press, New York, 2022
Distributed by Two Rivers Distribution

ISBN 978-1-62079-760-6 (hc)
ISBN 978-1-62097-768-2 (ebook)
CIP data is available

The New Press publishes books that promote and enrich public discussion and
understanding of the issues vital to our democracy and to a more equitable
world. These books are made possible by the enthusiasm of our readers; the
support of a committed group of donors, large and small; the collaboration
of our many partners in the independent media and the not-for-profit sector;
booksellers, who often hand-sell New Press books; librarians; and above all by
our authors.

www.thenewpress.com

Book design and composition by Bookbright Media
This book was set in Sabon and Oswald

Printed in the United States of America

Contents

Foreword by Angela Y. Davis | *ix*

Introduction | *1*

Vietnam and Laos | 21

9/11 and Afghanistan | 43

Iraq | 99

Libya | 151

Fragilities of U.S. Power | 177

Afterword | 195

Notes | *207*

Foreword

For almost as long as I can remember, Noam Chomsky has served as the conscience of a country whose government consistently engages with those parts of the world outside its own sphere of influence by either deploying violence or threatening to do so. Even when we in the United States have endured profound domestic crises, Chomsky has always insisted that we also turn our attention outwards, to avoid capitulating to the assumption that the nation-state, within whose boundaries we happen to live, is the most important political presence of our lives. He has always counseled us to reject American exceptionalism. His germinal essay "The Responsibility of Intellectuals" resonates today more than ever, especially as we collectively make great efforts to address a range of questions regarding the ways racism—and indeed racial capitalism—has structured the social, political, and cultural institutions that define our collective lives in the U.S. He reminds us that there is a geopolitical and historical context to this work. As his collaborator

Vijay Prashad also insists, the impact of colonialism and the role of the slave trade and slavery in the development of capitalism have had lasting effects not only in the U.S. but indeed throughout the world.

Although I have been reading Noam Chomsky for decades and have attended his lectures on too many occasions to count, my first opportunity to meet him in person was not until December 2012 when he, Vijay, and I participated in a program at the Berklee College of Music organized by Rachel Herzing and Isaac Ontiveros, representing Critical Resistance (CR). This event was a fundraiser benefiting CR, the LGBTQI prison abolitionist organization Black and Pink, and the City School in Boston, which develops youth leadership for social justice. I retain a particularly vivid memory of this event because just days earlier I came down with a nasty case of the flu and seriously wondered whether I should make the trip to Boston. (Given our experience with the COVID-19 pandemic over the last two years, I now realize I should have probably stayed at home.) But my sense then was that I could not miss the opportunity to meet this historic figure, who had taught me and the world so much about the "responsibility of intellectuals." It was a phenomenal event, and though I have little memory of my own contributions, I remember being absolutely captivated by the evening's conversations that unfolded under the rubric "Radical Futures and Prospects for Freedom." Our discussion evoked the prison industrial complex as a discernible product of the post-slavery history of the U.S. and of global capitalism as it has developed since the 1980s, and the three of us talked about lessons for abolitionist resistance drawn from anti-imperialist struggles and prospects for the future of internationalism.

I was impressed, as I always am, not only by the immensity of Chomsky's command of history and analysis, especially regarding the incalculable wreckages originating with the U.S. military, but also by his unpretentious presence. On this cold Boston night, after the event and reception had concluded—I think it was close to 11 p.m.—he prepared to leave. Someone asked him about his ride and he responded that, as usual, he would find his way home by bus. Of course half of the people there then volunteered to drive him home. But he never thought of himself as so special as to merit this treatment.

Over the decades during which generations of scholars and activists have been influenced by Chomsky's books, interviews, and lectures—indeed he is our country's preeminent public intellectual—he has always attempted to bring to light the hidden violences, those that are so often assumed to be simply collateral consequences that hardly merit recognition. For instance, he often emphasizes the point that there is a vast discrepancy between the numbers of Vietnamese people who were actually killed during the war (2 million officially acknowledged, but probably 4 million in reality), and the diminished numbers inscribed in our historical memory (in polls and studies, people typically imagine only 100,000 killed as an average). This disturbing difference between fact and perception serves as an example of the ways in which the state-ordered, brazen slaughter of human life can be so cavalierly minimized under the impact of U.S. ideology.

This most recent collaboration with Vijay Prashad continues to explore the theme of ugly wars conducted by the United States. I have long appreciated Vijay's insistence on the need for people inside progressive circles to generate a sharper sense of our situatedness within global struggles. Through the structure of a deeply engaging conversation between two of our most important contemporary public intellectuals, we are urged to defy the inattention of the media to the disastrous damage inflicted in Afghanistan on life, land, and resources in the aftermath of the U.S. withdrawal and the connections to the equally avoidable and unnecessary wars on Iraq and Libya. Thank you, Noam and

Vijay, for this insightful book which emphasizes the continuities, across time and political parties, of official policies and practices that produce and reproduce these militaristic incursions and offers us the kind of internationalist perspective that is our best chance for the future the world needs.

—*Angela Y. Davis*

Introduction

The Legacy of Ugly Wars

On August 15, 2021, the United States military had to withdraw from Afghanistan after a twenty-year occupation. Little good remained in place as the Taliban entered Kabul and took control of what remained of the Afghan state. The death toll from this war is contested, but few dispute that a few hundred thousand people have perished under fire (a United Nations study found that at least 40 percent of civilians killed by air strikes were children). The Afghan Ministry of Public Health estimates that two-thirds of Afghans suffer from war-induced mental health troubles. Half of the population lives below the poverty line, and about 60 percent of the population remains illiterate. Few gains were made on these fronts.

Meanwhile, the Taliban found that the coffers in the Central Bank's offices in Kabul were empty; the reserves—$9.5 billion—sat in U.S. banks, from which they were now seized by the United States to pay off the families of victims of the

9/11 attack. During the U.S. occupation, Afghanistan relied for its revenues on foreign aid, 43 percent of Afghan GDP in 2020. This collapsed as the United States withdrew; the UN Development Programme calculates a drop in the GDP because of the loss of foreign aid to be 20 percent (2021) and then 30 percent in the following years. Meanwhile, the United Nations estimates that by the end of 2022 the country's per capita income may decline to nearly half of 2012 levels. It is estimated that 97 percent of the Afghan people will fall below the poverty line, with mass starvation a real possibility. It was telling that the last drone strike by the U.S. military on Afghan soil struck a car carrying ten people, including seven children and Zemari Ahmadi, who drove a car for Nutrition & Education International (a Pasadena, California–based charity). The U.S. military first suggested that Ahmadi was an ISIS member, and took two weeks to acknowledge that the Reaper drone had killed civilians; no troops have been punished for this crime.

This is the nature of the ugly wars of the United States.

In recent years, the United States has failed to accomplish any of the objectives of its wars. The United States entered Afghanistan with horrendous bombing and a lawless campaign of extraordinary rendition in October 2001 with the objective of ejecting the Taliban from the country; now, twenty years later, the Taliban is back. In 2003, two years after the United States unleashed a war in Afghanistan, it opened an illegal war against Iraq, which ultimately result-ed in the start of an unconditional withdrawal by the Unit-ed States in 2011 after the refusal of the Iraqi parliament to allow U.S. troops extralegal protections. As the United States withdrew from Iraq, it opened a terrible war against Libya in 2011, where—as discussed later—France was in the lead, Britain behind, and then the United States eventu-ally took over. This war resulted in the creation of chaos in the region.

Not one of these wars—Afghanistan, Iraq, Libya—resulted in the creation of a pro-U.S. government. Each of these wars created needless suffering for the civilian populations. Mil-lions of people had their lives disrupted, while hundreds of thousands of people lost their lives. What faith in humanity can now be expected from a young person in Jalalabad or in Sirte? Will they now turn inward, fearing that any possibili-ty of change has been stolen from them by the barbaric wars inflicted upon them and other residents of their countries?

There is no question that the United States continues to have the world's largest military and that by using its base structure and its aerial and naval power it can strike any country at any time. But what is the point of bombing a country if that violence attains no political ends? The United States used its advanced drones to assassinate Taliban leaders, but for each leader that it killed, another half-dozen have emerged. Besides, the men in charge of the Taliban now—including the cofounder of the Taliban and head of its political commission, Mullah Abdul Ghani Baradar—have been there from the start; it would never have been possible to decapitate the entire Taliban leadership. More than $2 trillion has been spent by the United States on this war, in which U.S. triumphalism reigned from the start.

In early statements after the U.S. withdrawal from his country, Mullah Baradar said that his government would focus its attention on the corruption endemic in Afghanistan. Meanwhile, stories spread across Kabul about ministers of the last U.S.-friendly Afghan government, led by former World Bank official Ashraf Ghani, who attempted to leave the country in cars filled with dollar bills, which was the money that had been provided by the United States to Afghanistan supposedly for aid and infrastructure. The drain of wealth from the aid given to the country has been significant. In a 2016 report by the U.S. government's Special Inspector General for Afghanistan Reconstruction

(SIGAR) relating to the "Lessons Learned from the U.S. Experience with Corruption in Afghanistan," the investigators write: "Corruption significantly undermined the U.S. mission in Afghanistan by damaging the legitimacy of the Afghan government, strengthening popular support for the insurgency, and channeling material resources to insurgent groups." SIGAR created a "gallery of greed," which listed U.S. contractors who had siphoned aid money and pocketed it through fraud. More than $2 trillion has been spent on the U.S. occupation of Afghanistan, but it went neither to provide relief nor to build the country's infrastructure. The money fattened the wallets of the rich in the United States, Pakistan, and Afghanistan.

Corruption at the very top of the government depleted morale below. The United States pinned its hopes on the training of 300,000 soldiers of the Afghan National Army (ANA), spending $88 billion on this pursuit. In 2019, a purge of "ghost soldiers" in the rolls—soldiers who did not exist—led to the loss of 42,000 troops; it is likely that the number was higher. Morale in the ANA has plunged over the past few years, with defections from the army to other forces escalating. Defense of the provincial capitals was also weak, with Kabul falling to the Taliban almost without a fight. To this end, the last defense minister of the

Ghani government, General Bismillah Mohammadi, commented on Twitter about the governments that have been in power in Afghanistan since late 2001, "They tied our hands behind our backs and sold the homeland. Damn the rich man [Ghani] and his people." This captures the popular mood in Afghanistan at the time the United States departed.

The Godfather

In each of these wars—Afghanistan, Iraq, Libya—the possibility of a negotiated settlement lingered at the edge of the conflict. In Afghanistan, the Taliban understood the gravity of a U.S. attack after 9/11 and made it clear on several occasions that it would be prepared to hand over Osama bin Laden and the al-Qaeda network to a third country. The Taliban had already experienced a small U.S. attack in 1998 against targets in Khost, so they were familiar with the awesome power of the United States military. Their plea for a settlement was rejected. Saddam Hussein's government understood in 1990 that it had made an error in invading Kuwait, and it wanted to cut a deal with the United States to exit Kuwait without total humiliation; all attempts by the Iraqis to negotiate their withdrawal were met with disdain by the United States, which bombed Iraq heavily in 1991.

That is why Saddam Hussein was eager to make every concession to the United States in the aftermath of 9/11, allowing more and more UN inspections—whose inspectors found no weapons of mass destruction—and offering every means for the United States to verify that Iraq had no ill intentions toward the United States. Once more, Washington set aside the pleas from Baghdad and proceeded with its campaign, called Shock and Awe. In Libya, the government was eager to accept a peace plan laid out by the African Union, whose mission was prevented from going to Tripoli by NATO bombing, and then when it went there during the bombing and Muammar Qaddafi accepted its terms, the rebels with their advantage of NATO allies refused to accept the peace deal. The evidence is clear that the United States simply did not want to seek any peace agreement or even a preemptive surrender. When the United States wants war, it gets a war.

There is a mafia quality to the way the United States has exercised its power, something that goes back to the days of the genocide against the indigenous peoples of North America, who tried to negotiate with the settlers but faced instead the machine gun. When Chief Tecumseh of the Shawnee tried to negotiate with Indiana governor William Henry

Harrison in 1811, the United States government used military force to chase Tecumseh to Canada; Harrison became the president of the United States, winning a reward for seizing the land. This attitude is rooted in a settler–colonial culture that expanded the initial Atlantic seaboard–based United States into the territory of Native American societies, seizing a third of Mexico, and then French and Russian territories in the Gulf Coast and California. Once the territorial United States had been established, all by the gun, the armies gathered to seize far-off archipelagoes and islands (Hawaii, Guam, Puerto Rico, Philippines) as well as to establish dominion through the 1823 Monroe Doctrine of the American hemisphere. During the U.S. war on the Philippines in 1898, General Jacob Smith ordered his troops to "kill everyone over the age of ten" and create a "howling wilderness." A half-century later, in Vietnam, a U.S. helicopter team painted the slogan "Death is our Business and Business is Good" on the side of their quarters. The landscape had to be pacified, or else destroyed. The ethos here was defined by Lyndon B. Johnson, the U.S. president, who said, "It's silly talking about how many years we will spend in the jungles of Vietnam when we could pave the whole country and put parking stripes on it and still be home by Christmas." The idea that the United States—a city on the hill (a phrase from the Bible used by John Winthrop in 1630 to describe his new country as a "beacon of hope" for the world)—had a right to define the destiny of the Americas and to export this attitude to other lands, especially in parts of Africa and Asia, derives from its settler–colonial history.

World War II devastated most advanced industrial countries—certainly Europe, Japan, and the USSR; the United States, in contrast, saw none of its industrial base impacted. In fact, the war production enhanced industry in the United States, and the U.S. financial surplus gave the dollar a divine character not available to any other currency, not even the pound sterling. It was in this context that the United States began to aggressively define the path for its allies in Europe and Japan as well as to use every means necessary to subordinate the decolonization movement and to demonize the USSR through the Cold War system, which was imposed largely by the United States. Coups and military interventions define the Cold War era, from the United States–led coup in Iran (1953) to the U.S. military intervention in Iraq (1991). During these forty years, the United States' force was somewhat held in check by the presence of the Soviet Union and its allies, as well as by the emergence of the Third World as a political force. Nonetheless, the United States operated in total disregard for international law; U.S. military and diplomatic power and the operation of multinational corporations domiciled in Europe, Japan, and the United States could not be checked.

The Godfather attitude expanded geometrically after the collapse of the USSR, when the United States' ruling elite understood that they were the sole superpower. Benchmarks for this new era were the U.S. war in Iraq (1991) and the creation of the World Trade Organization (1994), the former a pure exercise of U.S. military power and the latter an institution by which to capture countries in a trade framework that the United States hoped to dominate. The U.S. wars against Afghanistan (2001) and Iraq (2003) came with little consideration for world opinion, even less for the possibility of preventing war through negotiation. The United States, as first among unequals, felt that it needed to answer to nobody. That's the Godfather attitude. It is how we see the United States in this book.

The Godfather attitude is not irrational. It develops to protect the property, privileges, and power of the ruling elite in the United States and their closest allies in Europe, Japan, and a few other countries. They recognize that their advantages cannot be permanently secured by free competition, which is the overarching ideology of their "freemarket" society. Two kinds of economic threat occasionally appear: the

10

first is the movement of workers and peasants in countries that produce key raw materials who refuse to accept subhuman, suppressed wages that enable the entire commodity chain to keep costs down and profits up; and the second is when countries where technological advances take place threaten the monopoly power of European, Japanese, and U.S. multinational companies. The United States either uses violence itself or sanctions violence through its authorized agents (dictators and police chiefs) against the workers and peasants who rebel, and against the governments that they might create to fashion a different path forward. The United States pushes trade policies—particularly intellectual property rights laws—that prevent countries from advancing their scientific and technological capacity. If there is a move against the interests of the United States, then it uses its control over international institutions to sanction countries or uses violence to discipline them. This violence and these laws are rooted in the Godfather attitude, which is another way of talking about imperialism.

Dangerous Escalations

That the United States has had to withdraw from Afghanistan and to virtually withdraw from Iraq, as well as found itself unable to control the dynamic in Libya, comes alongside reversals of U.S.-led coups in Chile, Honduras, and Bolivia. The regime of the 1973 coup in Chile is being undone by the drafting of a new constitution and by the 2021 election of a post-coup political coalition. The 2009 coup in Honduras has been reversed by the 2021 election of the political forces that had been overthrown in the coup. The 2021 election in Bolivia of the leftist forces is a reversal of the 2019 coup against the government of Evo Morales. These reversals—and there are many others—are important to document, although we don't discuss them fully in this book.

The most dangerous escalation of our time is neither in Latin America nor in the belt that runs from Afghanistan to Libya; the most dangerous situation is the pressure campaign that the United States is leading against China and Russia. The U.S. war on Iraq (2003) and the credit crisis (2007–8), as well as the increasing polarization of society in the United States, have weakened the country's ability to act as it did after 1991. This weakness is illustrated by these withdrawals and coup reversals. But this weakness should not be interpreted as the demise of U.S. power or the end of the "American Century." The United States has great reservoirs of power—financial, military, diplomatic, cultural—which it will continue to wield for a long time yet. But the relative weakness of the United States made room for the emergence of China as an important world power.

In the long view, China has not "emerged" as a world power but is merely returning to a situation that prevailed two hundred years ago. Then, in 1820, China's economy was six times the size of Great Britain's, at the time the largest economy in Europe and a dominant maritime and imperial power, and it was twenty times the size of the United States' economy. The harsh edge of European imperialism, particularly British military aggression, destroyed China's economic strength and depleted its power within a generation. China struggled with conflict from the first Opium War of 1839 to the end of its civil war in 1949, over a hundred years of violence and despair. The Chinese Revolution came at the end of this cycle of violence. In 1949, Mao Zedong said, "The Chinese people have now stood up." This was a statement against what Chinese historians call a "century of humiliation." In 1978, the Chinese government opened the economy but put in place measures to import the latest science and technology. A few decades later, the improvements to human life in China and the adaptation and expansion of scientific knowledge and technological developments had helped improve the social conditions of the Chinese people; problems, of course, remain in China, including corruption and inequality, which require attention. It is this China, with technological advances that are well ahead of the West's firms, that poses not a military or security threat to the West but a threat to the idea that only the West can lead in certain sectors (telecommunications, robotics, high-speed rail, non-carbon energy). China, meanwhile, has exported its developments through the Belt and Road Initiative (BRI), which is a frontal challenge to the International Monetary Fund and its debt-driven forms of engagement with the Global South (through the Paris Club and the London Club, both of which now acknowledge that poorer countries prefer to borrow from Chinese banks than from them).

The worst case of the Godfather's behavior is the increasing provocative actions toward China. That's very dangerous. By now there's constant talk about what's called the "China threat." You even read about the terrible "China threat" in sober, usually reasonable journals. We are told that the United States must move expeditiously to contain and limit the China threat. What exactly is the China threat? That question is rarely raised in the United States. It is discussed in Australia, whose main trading partner is China. The rightist Australian leadership—not needing pressure from Washington—has been making its own moves to provoke China. It is in close alliance with former Australian prime minister Paul Keating, who looked at the "China threat" and concluded, realistically, that the China threat is China's existence. The United States will not tolerate the existence of a state that cannot be intimidated the way Europe can be intimidated, a state that therefore does not follow U.S. orders the way Europe does. China, which has developed its own powerful economy, pursues its own course. That's the "China threat."

What makes the power of the United States so fragile now is not merely its own weaknesses, but that it is weakened in the context of the emergence of China and China's alliance with Russia. A new dangerous escalation is taking place around Eurasia to prevent China's influence from spreading out of its borders and to threaten Russia if it insists on operating along with China as a separate pole in international affairs. Russia's war in Ukraine is a consequence—partly—of this pressure campaign. It is in this context that we talk in this book about the two forms of international relations: the U.S. form of a "rules-based order," which means that the world must follow the U.S.-imposed rules, or the UN form of an international order based on the UN Charter (1945). The Godfather would like the world to adopt its rules, whereas the world is keener to build procedures that are rooted in the document that has the greatest consensus of any document ever, which is the United Nations Charter. One of the undercurrents of this book is our insistence on measuring the behavior of the Godfather according to international law, which is typically informed by the UN Charter. We are not naïve about the limitations of the UN Charter or of the UN system, but it is important to acknowledge that 193 countries have signed on to the charter, which is a binding treaty and the basis for much of the international law that follows it.

Our Book

The Withdrawal is based on conversations between the two of us held in late 2021, but also on conversations we have had over the course of the past few years. The book is an edited version of these conversations, drawing as they do from our various investigations and writings. We are grateful to Marc Favreau of The New Press for initiating the idea of this book, and to our various publishers around the world for their editions of *The Withdrawal*. Thanks to Daniel Tirado of Tricontinental: Institute for Social Research for technical help.

In 2012, Noam had a conversation with Angela Davis, moderated by Vijay, in Boston. It was striking that this was the first time that Angela and Noam had met in person. The conversation's theme was "Radical Futures," a phrase that resonates a decade later. This book brings the three of us back together again, with Angela's foreword as a guide into the argument.

THE WITHDRAWAL

1

Vietnam and Laos

VIJAY: The air is calm in Caracas (Venezuela). On the night-stand are sitting two books that became central to my reading habits about thirty years ago: Noam Chomsky's *American Power and the New Mandarins* (1969) and *The Backroom Boys* (1973). Both reflect on the atrocious U.S. war against the people of Vietnam, both are on the bureaucrats (the "new mandarins" and the "backroom boys") who prosecute these wars in the name of "democracy" and "human rights." You know where Chomsky stands if you just glance at the dedication to *American Power*: "To the brave young men who refuse to serve in a criminal war." That was a clear statement of principle, one that has remained the dedication to each of Noam's books over the course of the past half-century and more. He has consistently stood with the people against the social forces that are committed to the expansion of their property, their power, and their privileges. I'm reading these two early political classics by Chomsky in preparation for a long conversation we are about to have about the withdrawal of the United States from Afghanistan, Iraq, and Libya, but really about the slow attrition of U.S. power and the U.S. hybrid war that has emerged against China and Russia. I want to be sure I am prepared when I talk to Noam because he—into his

23

mid-nineties—remains sharp and ready, an intellectual shadow boxer of the highest caliber.

Noam's *American Power* is anchored by the essay "The Responsibility of Intellectuals." It was delivered in 1966 at Harvard University's Hillel (the Jewish student organization). The essay dazzles, with Noam piercing the hypocrisies of the intellectual world of the United States, where professors rest smugly on the ideals of American civilization but rarely confront its reality. "Intellectuals are in a position to expose the lies of governments, to analyze actions according to their causes and motives and often hidden intentions," wrote Noam, in essence laying out the methodology for the critical intellectual. What motivates these reflections is the brazenness of men such as Arthur Schlesinger, a Harvard University professor who was President John F. Kennedy's favorite intellectual and advisor. After the 1961 U.S.-planned invasion of Cuba by right-wing exiles—the Bay of Pigs fiasco—Schlesinger, who smugly placed himself at the "vital center" of U.S. politics, lied to the press about the assault on Cuba. At the time of the publication of Schlesinger's book *A Thousand Days* (1965), he was asked about the lying, and he said plainly that he had lied, that's it. Noam saw this exchange in the *New York Times* around the time that Schlesinger was offered the Albert Schweitzer Professorship in the Humanities at the City University of New York. In "The Responsibility of Intellectuals," Noam wrote of this casual deceit and the praise it elicited from the establishment in the United States: "It is of no particular interest that one man is quite happy to lie on behalf of a cause which he knows to be unjust; but it is significant that such events provoke so little response in the intellectual community— no feeling, for example, that there is something strange in the offer of a major chair in humanities to a historian who feels it is to be his duty to persuade the world that an American-sponsored invasion of a near-by country is nothing of the sort."

By the time Noam gave that talk at Harvard's Hillel Society, he was already a leading linguist based on a powerful review of B.F. Skinner's *Verbal Behavior* (in *Language*, 1959), on four published books (*Syntactic Structures*, 1957; *Current Issues in Linguistic Theory*, 1964; *Aspects of the Theory of Syntax*, 1965; *Cartesian Linguistics*, 1965), and on several widely circulated papers. Years later, in *The Cold War and the University* (1997), three important scholars in the sciences (Chomsky from linguistics, Richard Lewontin from biology, and Ray Siever from geology) argued that when most administrations participated in the attack on the left within the academy during the 1950s and 1960s, they avoided attacking science faculty, who were often seen as technocrats; his linguistics research and reputation, Noam pointed out, is what afforded him a perch from which to develop a powerful critical voice within the U.S. academy.

In 1963, some of the luminaries of the New York publishing world started the *New York Review of Books*. While the early issues reflected the elite world of publishing, the editors opened their pages to more radical voices as the social movements began to fill the streets of the United States. One of those voices, from 1967 ("The Responsibility of Intellectuals") to 1975 ("The Meaning of Vietnam"), was Noam; he wrote some of the finest pieces about the U.S. war on Vietnam, Laos, and Cambodia, indeed some of the best writing on the war published in the United States.

Noam, tell me about that landmark essay of yours called "The Responsibility of Intellectuals."

NOAM: Well, actually, "The Responsibility of Intellectuals" was first published in a Harvard University journal, *Mosaic*, the journal of the Hillel Society. They must have destroyed it from their archives by now, I'm sure. It was picked up by the *New York Review of Books*, which at that time had a coterie of leftist writers. The editors were following the developments among young intellectuals who in the late 1960s were becoming involved in activist movements. So, they published this essay and others on resistance. That period ended in the early 1970s with the move toward reaction. But I can't say I felt anything particular about it. I was too involved in the antiwar movement to think about anything else. It was most of my life at that time. We were then involved in resistance activities. I was facing a probable long prison sentence at this time.

VIJAY: In 1967, you drafted a "Call to Resist" with Paul Lauter and others, which was published in several outlets. Article 9 of the "Call" notes, "We call upon all men of good will to join us in this confrontation with immoral authority. Especially we call upon universities to fulfil their mission of enlightenment and religious organizations to honor their heritage of brotherhood. Now is the time to resist." It was based on this call and the actions that it provoked that you—along with Dr. Benjamin Spock and William Sloane Coffin—found yourselves in

the crosshairs of the U.S. government. I remember reading the essay you wrote with Paul Lauter and Florence
Howe about the Boston "conspiracy trial," in which you
wrote that the United Nations Charter, the Nuremberg
Principles, and the U.S. Constitution laid a pretty good
foundation to "encourage resistance" ("Reflections on a
Political Trial," *New York Review of Books*, August 22,
1968). The basis for that encouragement was put clearly
in the article: "It is impossible to conduct a brutal war of
aggression in the name of an enlightened and informed
citizenry; either the war must be terminated, or democratic rights, including the right to information and free
discussion, must be restricted. This is true not only of the
war in Vietnam, but also of the use of American force
to intervene in the internal affairs of other countries."
Four of the five defendants had been found guilty and
sentenced. It is important to recall that President Lyndon
Johnson's attorney general, Ramsey Clark, decided not to
prosecute the young men who were burning their draft
cards but instead to go after Dr. Benjamin Spock; Rev-
erend William Sloane Coffin, chaplain of Yale; Marcus
Raskin, founder of the Institute for Policy Studies; and
others, so that the war could be "vigorously debated,"
as Clark later put it. You were in the queue for prosecu-

tion as part of this so-called conspiracy. This essay with Lauter and Howe, along with an essay called "On Resistance" (*New York Review of Books*, December 7, 1967), defines your attitude toward the U.S. war, grounded—as you say—in the UN Charter and the U.S. Constitution. These two texts, and others, have provided you with the foundation to offer a strong critique of U.S. power, particularly military power. I know you're going to dismiss this question, but I'll ask it anyway: From where have you been able to marshal the courage to stand up—sometimes by yourself—and say the things that you say?

NOAM: You can't raise the question of courage about people as privileged as I am. You want to look at courage, go to the peasants fighting for their lives in southern Colombia, or the courage of the Kurds in eastern Turkey, or the Palestinians in the refugee camps and in the occupied territories. Places where you—as a journalist—have spent most of your life. There, you can talk about courage. Not for people like me.

VIJAY: Let me persist a bit. Leave courage out of it. What about resilience? I mean, at some point, have you felt, *Ah, forget it. This is not worthwhile.* You seem to persist and

29

persist with the same kind of dedication despite the terrible attacks. I want to try to understand that a little bit. An aunt of mine said, "Noam Chomsky is a long-distance runner." I feel that this is an accurate statement. Why have you not given up the race?

NOAM: It probably goes back to an unattractive personal trait: arrogance. If I'm going to be bitterly condemned by the whole intellectual community, but if I think I'm right, I don't care.

VIJAY: I like that answer a lot. I think that's beautiful. I wouldn't call it arrogance. I would call it—perhaps—stubbornness. You know, sometimes reality forces us to be stubborn.

NOAM: Maybe. Call it what you want. There was a time when it got serious enough that my first wife, Carol, who died some years ago, went back to college after seventeen years because it looked as if she'd have to support the family. It was very likely that I would get a prison sentence. In fact, I was designated by the prosecutor in the first trial of the resistance to be the person in the next trial who would be charged. It looked as if the trials would go through. We were actually saved by real courage: the

Tet Offensive. The Tet Offensive took place in January 1968. You don't discuss it much in the West, but this was the most amazing uprising in human history. I mean, the South Vietnamese countryside was saturated with about six hundred thousand U.S. troops and another seven hundred thousand to eight hundred thousand troops of the Saigon army. Every village was penetrated with informants from Saigon and the United States everywhere. No one had a clue that this uprising was going to take place all across the country. I don't think that there is anything in history that comes anywhere close to this. It was an amazing shock in the United States. The U.S. leadership was listening to the generals say, "It's all under control. We will win any time." Tet rattled this assessment. The U.S. government was forced to shift its position. There was a group called the Wise Men, Wall Street lawyers and backroom boys, who met and basically informed Johnson that he was not going to run again. They told him that he had to move toward the beginnings of some kind of negotiation and partial withdrawal. One part of this new situation was to make an effort to make peace with the young people who were protesting across the United States. If you take a look at the last part of the Pentagon Papers, the part that nobody reads that comes right after the Tet Offensive, it says that there was a discussion about sending more troops. But the joint chiefs were not eager. They said, "If you send more troops, we're going to need them for civil disorder control in the United States. Women, young people: they're going to be revolting all over the place. We can't send more troops abroad." That's the last couple of pages of the Pentagon Papers. There was real concern about this, and they called off the trials of the resistance. So, I was never tried.

VIJAY: You are right about the lack of information about, let alone knowledge of, the Tet Offensive. It is probably a good idea to say a little more about that turning point in the politics of the U.S. war. Late at night on January 30, 1968, tens of thousands of soldiers from the National Liberation Front of South Vietnam (Viet Cong) and the People's Army of Vietnam began a series of coordinated attacks on the army of the dictatorship of Saigon (ARVN) as well as on the U.S. armed forces and various allies. Since the attacks came on the holiday of Tet Nguyen Dan, many soldiers of the ARVN were on leave and morale was generally low. What was incredible was that the attack took place in thirty-six of the forty-four provincial capi-tals in more than one hundred towns and cities. In the

U.S. government reports that had been compiled as the *Report of the Office of the Secretary of Defense: Vietnam Task Force*, later leaked and called the Pentagon Papers, it was clear that the Tet Offensive rattled the confidence of the war planners in Washington. President Lyndon Johnson was "deeply shaken" by the recommendation from his war cabinet that the United States should consider a withdrawal. Even though the United States and ARVN regained the advantage after an initial rebuff, it was clear that they would not prevail over the communists in both halves of Vietnam. As a result of the Tet Offensive, Johnson ended the bombardment of North Vietnam and declined to run for a second term; Hanoi meanwhile called for negotiations to begin in May 1968, a process that would end with the U.S. withdrawal in 1975.

That meeting of the Wise Men—which you mentioned —took place on March 25, 1968; it shook President Johnson, and also some members of his team. It was an ugly meeting. General Earle Wheeler, a consummate hawk who was the chair of the Joint Chiefs of Staff, argued to increase troop deployments and deepen the U.S. war, but the realities in Saigon impacted even his will. "In late February," Wheeler reported to this meeting of the Wise Men, "I visited South Vietnam. At that time, the situation was fluid. The South Vietnamese were shook and had a variety of paralysis. Government and military were clustered in urban areas to protect against a second wave of attacks. I told President [Nguyen Van] Thieu that the South Vietnam forces had to go on the offensive. Thieu said South Vietnam could not take another Tet offensive." The Wise Men had brutal tricks up their sleeves, but even they sniffed the air and found that reality had defeated them. "The use of atomic weapons is unthinkable," said National Security Advisor McGeorge Bundy, as if weighing their possible use against a population already bombed brutally. For comparison, the United States dropped three times as many bombs by weight on Vietnam than were dropped in both the European and Pacific theaters of World War II; the explosive impact of the ordinance dropped on Vietnam was a hundred times the combined impact of the Hiroshima and Nagasaki atom bombs. Senior U.S. State Department official George Ball commented gingerly, "As long as we continue to bomb, we alienate ourselves from the civilized world. A bombing halt would quieten the situation here at home." It was Ball's attitude—to preserve the U.S. reputation and to prevent the acceleration of civil unrest within the United States—that prevailed for Johnson. Nixon tried to escalate the conflict, with Wheeler coming up with the Vietnamization policy, but this was futile. It was already clear that the United States had lost the war and would have to withdraw.

A year after the publication of *American Power*, you went to Vietnam with two of your friends, Doug Dowd, a professor of economics at Cornell University, and Richard Fernandez, a minister in the United Church of Christ. You went to Hanoi (including offering a course of lectures at the Polytechnic University) and to the countryside outside Hanoi. All of this is described in detail in *At War with Asia* (1970). A few years ago, the Australian scholar Kevin Hewison asked you about this 1970 visit, and this is what you said:

NOAM: North Vietnam was interesting, but I didn't see much. I was mostly lecturing at the Polytechnic University—more accurately, in the ruins of the university. There was a bombing pause, so faculty and students could be brought back from the countryside. They had been out of touch with the world for five years. I spent every day lecturing on any topic I could think of and that I knew anything about. There were all kinds of questions and interest, from international affairs to linguistics and philosophy to what's Norman Mailer doing these days and so on. I did get around a little bit, but not very far from Hanoi. You could see evidence of U.S. bombing in Hanoi. With my group of visitors—Doug Dowd and Dick Fernandez—we traveled a bit beyond Hanoi and were able to see the wreckage of Phu Ly, the hospital destroyed in Thanh Hoa city, which the United States claimed was never hit, but we could see the shell. The area around Ham Rong Bridge had been intensively bombed. It was a kind of moonscape. Villages, everything, just totally destroyed, and the bridge barely standing. But we knew that Hanoi was somewhat protected because there were embassies, foreign correspondents. The further you got from Hanoi, the more intensive the bombing.

VIJAY: The United States conducted a "secret" bombing campaign against Laos from 1964 to 1973 to support the Royal Lao regime against the Pathet Lao and to prevent the alleged use of Laos by the Vietnamese to resupply lines in the south of Vietnam. The United States conducted 580,000 bombing missions, dropping a full payload of bombs every eight minutes around the clock for nine years. The country is considered the most bombed on the planet. You traveled in Laos with Fred Branfman, who directed Project Air War and lived in Laos. Branfman, you recalled, "had been trying desperately to get somebody to pay attention to what was going on."

NOAM: I was able to spend several days visiting refugee camps about thirty kilometers or so away from Vientiane, and also to meet many people I would never have been able to locate on my own. All of which I wrote about, though sometimes protecting the identity of people in severe danger. It was the right time to be there. The CIA mercenary army had shortly before cleared out tens of thousands of people from northern Laos—from the Plain of Jars—where many of them had been living in caves for years, subjected to what was, at that time, the most intensive bombing in history, soon to be surpassed in Cambodia. I spent a lot of time interviewing these refugees, which was revealing.

One of the other interesting things I did on this trip related to the story of the time that claimed North Vietnam had fifty thousand troops in Laos and that's why the United States had to bomb. I was interested in the sources and did what seemed to be the obvious thing: I went to the American embassy and asked to speak to the political officer—typically, the CIA representative at the embassy. He came down and was very friendly, and I asked him if I could see some of the background material on the reported fifty thousand troops. He took me up to a room and gave me piles of documentation. He also said that I was the first person to ever ask him for background, which was interesting. I read through it, and I found that there was evidence that there was one Vietnamese battalion of maybe 2,500 people somewhere up in northern Laos, and the rest of the so-called 50,000 were either invented or were old men carrying a bag of rice on their back trying to make it through the bombing. This information was astonishing, because at this time the United States was already using a forward base in northern Laos to guide the bombing of North Vietnam, so my guess was that there would have been a lot more North Vietnamese than that around. This information was corroborated then by the reports of interviews with captured prisoners and other material that I reviewed. Some of this material was provided by Fred Branfman and some I was able to find as I saw a bit more of the country—not much, but some. This visit to Laos was a very moving experience. There had been some reporting of the so-called secret war. Jacques Decornoy had had an article in *Le Monde* and freelance journalist Tim Allman had written about it. So, there was scattered material, but I was able to see evidence in some depth that hadn't appeared. I guess of any of the things I've ever written, that was the one that was closest to my feelings. I usually try to keep my feelings out of what I write, but I probably didn't in that one.

VIJAY: Your article in the *New York Review of Books*—"A Visit to Laos" (July 23, 1970)—is a model of careful reporting based on a range of conversations with refugees and peasants as well as CIA officials. The last paragraph captures a little of your wistfulness, "When I arrived in Laos and found young Americans living there, out of free choice, I was surprised. After only a week, I began to have a sense of the appeal of the country and its people—along with despair about its future." The bombing of Laos lasted another three years; the war on Vietnam lasted another five years.

These days, in Caracas, the mood is more confident than it was in 2018–2020, when it appeared as if the United States might intervene militarily to overthrow the Bolivarian Revolution. Reading *The Backroom Boys* in this context suggested to me the flexibleness of the U.S. project. If the U.S. project fails to attain its objective in one place, it shifts its focus to another, not always fully along the lines of a grand strategy. The second essay in the book, "Endgame" (first published in *Ramparts*, April 1973), argues that even if "Western force actually is withdrawn from Indochina . . . the struggle will quickly be joined elsewhere." These are "inevitable conflicts," you wrote. Two years later, when the United States withdrew from Vietnam, you published a brief comment in the *New York Review of Books* ("The Meaning of Vietnam," June 12, 1975), which closes with the following thoughts:

The U.S. government was unable to subdue the forces of revolutionary nationalism in Indochina, but the American people are a less resilient enemy. If the apologists for state violence succeed in reversing their ideological defeats of the past years, the stage will be set for a renewal of armed intervention in the case of "local subversion or rebellion" that threatens to extricate some region from the U.S.-dominated global system. A prestigious study group twenty years ago identified the primary threat of "communism" as the economic transformation of the communist powers "in ways which reduce their willingness and ability to complement the industrial economies of the West." The American effort to contain this threat in Indochina was blunted, but the struggle will doubtless continue elsewhere. Its issue will be affected,

40

if not determined, by the outcome of the ideological conflict over "the lessons of Vietnam."

When the United States lost in Vietnam, it shifted focus—now looking toward Central Asia, where the backroom boys wanted to provoke the USSR, and to Central America, where the Contras became President Ronald Reagan's freedom fighters. Names from that era—Elliot Abrams first among them—were resurrected to haunt the people of Venezuela as they haunted Nicaragua and El Salvador decades ago.

In the lobby of the Venezuelan foreign ministry there is a statue of Salvador Allende's eyeglasses. This is a sculpture done by the Chilean artist Carlos Altamirano. The eyeglasses are broken, as they were found after the coup of 1973 by General Augusto Pinochet. They are a constant reminder of the Godfather's coups, as seen from the standpoint of its victims.

2

9/11 and Afghanistan

VIJAY: After the Tet Offensive in 1968, General Earle Wheeler developed a policy called Vietnamization, namely, to use Vietnamese troops under Saigon's flag to prosecute a war that the United States was not willing to shed more blood over (this was a policy borrowed from the French, who called it *jaunissement*, or "yellowing," as early as 1943). This policy of Vietnamization, developed in 1968, would be adopted in Central Asia and Central America to bleed parts of the world to ensure that the United States maintained primacy and that the USSR would be weakened. As the United States developed its "yellowing" policy, a series of left-leaning revolutions took place almost to validate the backroom boys' fantasy of dominos falling to communism:

Guinea-Bissau, September 1974
Vietnam, April 1975
Laos, May 1975
Mozambique, June 1975
Cape Verde, July 1975
São Tome, July 1975
Afghanistan, April 1978
Grenada, March 1979
Nicaragua, July 1979
Zimbabwe, April 1980

Several of these revolutions took place in Portuguese colonies through armed struggle and mass mobilization; because of the gruesome wars prosecuted by the Portuguese, the fascist state—the *Estado Novo* of António Salazar—fell in the homeland. Armed struggle defined the victories not only in these colonies, but also in Vietnam, Laos, Nicaragua, and Zimbabwe. Afghanistan and Grenada were the result of conventional coups d'état. These were anti-colonial struggles with a socialist character. One more key mass upsurge in this period—that in Iran—resulted in the formation of a theocratic order, one that was not socialist but equally determined to resist U.S. interference and domination. Against the leftist project in Afghanistan, the United States "yellowed" the war by large-scale recruitment of reactionary forces from Afghanistan and Pakistan, funded by Saudi petrodollars and armed to the teeth by the CIA and other U.S. agencies, as well as given logistical support by the religiously committed military dictatorship in Pakistan.

What was done against the leftist project in Afghanistan was replicated in Central America with the Contras (in Nicaragua) and with the death squads of El Salvador, Guatemala, and Honduras. In 1986, at the height of the U.S.-driven proxy wars in Central America and Central

Asia, you went on *10 O'clock News* to debate John Silber, the president of Boston University and a member of Henry Kissinger's commission to exaggerate the threat of communism in Central America. In this discussion, you bluntly described the nature of the Contras, which might as well have been the U.S.-backed Mujahideen in Pakistan–Afghanistan:

NOAM: As even the most ardent supporters of the Contras now concede, this is what they call a proxy army, which is attacking Nicaragua from foreign bases, is entirely dependent on its masters for directions and support, has never put forth a political program, has created no base of political support within the country, and almost its entire top military command is Somozist officers [officers of the regime of Anastasio Somoza, who was overthrown by the Nicaraguan Revolution]. Its military achievements so far consist of a long and horrifying series of very well-documented torture, mutilation, and atrocities, and essentially nothing else. U.S. administration officials are now openly conceding in public that the main function of the Contras is to retard or reverse the rate of social reform in Nicaragua and to try to terminate the openness of that society. The state of siege, for example, which

47

was imposed last fall [1985], and which is very mild, I should say—there is much political opening in Nicaragua, as everyone there up to the American ambassador will tell you—that corresponds roughly to the state of siege which has been in place in El Salvador since early 1980, except in El Salvador it has been associated with a huge massacre of tens of thousands of people. Destruction of the press, so on and so forth. Whereas in Nicaragua it is a reaction to a war that we are carrying out against them with precisely the purpose of trying to retard social reform and to restrict the possibilities of an open and developing society. That is a cruel and savage policy, which we should terminate.

VIJAY: In 2004, you described the Mujahideen in much the same way as you spoke about the Contras:

NOAM: The United States went beyond supporting the Mujahideen. They organized them. They collected radical Islamists from around the world, the most violent, crazed elements they could find, and tried to forge them into a military force in Afghanistan. You could argue that would have been legitimate if it had been for the purpose of defending Afghanistan. But it wasn't. In fact, it probably prolonged the war in Afghanistan. It looks from the Russian archives as though they were ready to pull out in the early 1980s, and this prolonged the war. But that wasn't the point. The point was to harm the Russians, not to defend the Afghans. So, the Mujahideen were carrying out terrorist activities right inside Russia, based in Afghanistan. Incidentally, those terrorist activities stopped after the Russians pulled out of Afghanistan, because what they were trying to do is just what they say, in their terminology, protect Muslim lands from the infidels. When the infidels pulled out, they stopped carrying out terrorist attacks in Russia from Afghanistan. Islamists were brought to Afghanistan. They were armed, trained, directed by Pakistani intelligence mainly, but under CIA supervision and control, with the support of Britain and other powers, for the purpose of trying to harm the Russians as much as possible at that time. And, yes, they morphed into what became al-Qaeda. Eqbal Ahmad recognized right away and warned—a lonely voice—that the United States and its allies were creating a terrorist monster, reviving concepts of "jihad" as "holy war" that had been dormant for centuries in the Islamic world.

VIJAY: It was these Contras and the Mujahideen that were
the instrument of U.S. policy. Certainly, they weakened
the possibility for the states in Central Asia and Central America to build functioning societies, forcing these
countries to pay an enormous social penalty. Out of the
detritus of these wars emerged narco-traffickers, terrorists, mafias, and other social threats. Al-Qaeda is a product of this ugly soup. The attack on the United States on
9/11 was what the CIA called blowback, a term from
physics that precisely describes in the world of politics the
unintended consequences of deliberate policies. What the
Mujahideen and the Contras became was not a surprise to
those who had long warned about the social character of
U.S. policy in these regions. This is an important point of
your book *9/11*, published in November 2001 as a warning about the rush to destroy Afghanistan based on a syn-
optic history of U.S. violence in similar circumstances. On
September 11, 2001, al-Qaeda struck the United States
through spectacular terrorist attacks. The U.S. president,
George W. Bush, immediately rushed his country to a war
footing, making it clear that Afghanistan was the target.
On October 7, 2001, the United States began to bomb
Afghanistan.

Was the twenty-year war that the United States prosecuted against the Afghan people a criminal war, as you called the war on Vietnam? First, was it criminal in that it was a case of conscious and premeditated aggression? Second, was the conduct of the war itself an indescribable atrocity?

NOAM: It was not criminal on the scale of Indochina, which was an incredible crime. But yet, it was unprovoked, it was an illegitimate aggression, and it was a severe atrocity. If you go back twenty years, you can find what I wrote then, no longer in the *New York Review of Books* but now in small journals (such as *Z Magazine*). The United States had no basis whatsoever for invading Afghanistan. 9/11 took place; it was assumed that it was probably carried out by al-Qaeda and Osama bin Laden, who were in Afghanistan, but the Taliban weren't responsible for what he might have done. And, certainly, the people of Afghanistan weren't responsible. Right after 9/11, the U.S. government initiated an intense international investigation, probably the most intense and extreme in history. Eight months later, Robert Mueller, the head of the FBI, gave his first extensive press conference. This is eight months after the United States invaded. Mueller was asked, of course, "What do you know about 9/11?" He said that we

51

assume that it was probably carried out by al-Qaeda, but we haven't been able to establish it yet. That's eight months after the invasion. If the United States had been interested in getting hold of al-Qaeda and bin Laden, at that time a small group probably on the Afghanistan–Pakistan border, they could have carried it out with a small police operation, probably with the cooperation of the Taliban, who had every reason to get rid of this irritant. They couldn't expel al-Qaeda and bin Laden because of the nature of tribal culture, but they didn't want them around. They were just an irritant for them. And the Taliban made several tentative offers of extradition to Islamic states, where the United States could have quickly picked them up. In fact, a couple weeks after the U.S. invasion, the Taliban offered a complete surrender, total surrender, which means al-Qaeda and bin Laden would have been in U.S. hands. The U.S. response was, "We do not negotiate surrenders." Donald Rumsfeld, U.S. secretary of defense at the time, echoed immediately by George W. Bush, said, "We don't negotiate surrenders. We have bigger aims than that." The aim was sketched out by Rumsfeld himself in some of his notes, but also by General Wesley Clark, who said he had seen the detailed proposals for how the U.S. planned to expand its—he didn't call it aggression, but

I will—its aggression into seven countries in the region. These countries were Iran, Iraq, Libya, Lebanon, Somalia, Sudan, and Syria. Clark said this in a television interview in 2007. This was just the first step. President Bush was asked subsequently in a press conference, "What do you know about bin Laden?" He said, "We don't really care. We're not much interested."

A couple of weeks after 9/11, the United States cut off aid supplies from Pakistan. Afghanistan was suffering then under severe humanitarian threat. Millions of people were facing potential starvation. The United States cut off all truck traffic from Pakistan to Afghanistan, the main source of aid, just to starve the Afghan people. Other similar measures were carried out. Aid groups were infuriated, were pleading for restoration of just plain aid to millions of Afghans who were on the edge of starvation. Nobody cared. Nothing. It was barely even reported. They got a line or two here and there in the *New York Times*, or just got casually referred to. And meanwhile the United States began its invasion.

So, why did the United States invade in the first place? Well, the only serious response I've heard to that, and I think the correct one, was given by Abdul Haq, the most respected figure in the anti-Taliban Afghan resistance. Haq gave an interview in mid-October 2001 to Anatol Lieven, a respected scholar of Central Asia. Lieven asked Haq, "Why do you think the U.S. invaded?" Haq answered, "The United States doesn't care about the Afghan people. They know they're going to kill plenty of Afghans. They're going to undermine our efforts to overthrow the Taliban from within." Which, Abdul Haq thought, was possible. But the United States didn't care. The U.S. government wanted to show its muscle and intimidate everyone. That's Rumsfeld—"We don't negotiate surrenders. We just want to show our muscle, intimidate everyone, go on to further goals." If you can think of a better answer than that, I'd like to hear it. I've never heard a better one. I think that's why the United States dismissed the Taliban surrender claims. They simply didn't care about gaining control over al-Qaeda and bin Laden, or whatever they were. Just wasn't a major interest. And as I said, they didn't even know that they were responsible for 9/11 at the time.

VIJAY: In February 2002, you wrote an article that assessed the early period of the U.S. war on Afghanistan ("The War in Afghanistan," Z *Magazine*, February 1, 2002). In that article, you wrote about the "belated concern about the fate of women in Afghanistan, even reaching the First Lady," Laura Bush, who had made a syrupy radio address about how the U.S. war would help Afghan women. "The fight against terrorism is also a fight for the rights and dignity of women," she said, which was fine as an abstract sentiment, but which meant nothing in practice. You rightly said that this was a concern that was not shared for women elsewhere in Central and South Asia, certainly not in Saudi Arabia and the Gulf states. "No sane person advocates foreign military intervention to rectify these and other injustices," you wrote, although this was the basis for many liberals to support the war. You pointed to the work of the Revolutionary Association of the Women of Afghanistan (RAWA), which had called for "the eradication of the plague of Taliban and al-Qaeda," but not through the agency of the U.S. warlords, whose "record of human rights violations" is "as bad as that of the Taliban." By the time you wrote your essay, it was clear that the U.S. warlords were in power and that the situation of women in Afghanistan would not improve. I had met with Anahita Ratebzad, a communist who was exiled in Germany, to talk about these matters. She had been one of the founders of the Democratic Organization of Afghan Women (DOAW) in 1965, and one of four women elected to parliament that year. At the time of the communist coup in 1978, the literacy rate in the country was a mere 18.6 percent (the numbers for women were negligible). In 1978–79, eighteen thousand instructors—many from DOAW—went into rural and urban areas to hasten the people's literacy, which was seen as the necessary foundation for any social reform. Hundreds of women left colleges each year as teachers and as doctors, as government officials and as professors. They took the ideas that had been developed in Kabul and brought them to rural areas, where they directly confronted the tribal leaders, the landlords, and the clergy. It was these rural literacy instructors—again, many of them women—who were the initial target of the U.S.-backed warlords, who attacked and murdered thousands of instructors from their Pakistani bases. All of this was not registered in the public debate. Nor, later in 2003, did the international press pay much attention to the words of Malalai Joya, who—as an elected member of the *loya jirga* (the effective parliament)—said of those in the hall with her that "they were the most anti-women people in the society" and that "they should be taken to national and international court." The head of the *loya jirga*, Sibghatullah Mojaddedi, regarded by the United States as a "moderate," called Malalai Joya an "infidel" and a "communist" and had her removed from the *jirga*. These were the men who came to power on the wings of F-16s.

When you were writing *9/11*, you encountered Rasil Basu, who had worked with the United Nations in Afghanistan and knew of the developments that immediately preceded the warlord and Taliban era of Afghanistan. What was she telling you in the lead-up to the U.S. war on Afghanistan?

NOAM: It's a very interesting story. Rasil Basu was a highly regarded international feminist figure who worked mostly for the United Nations. She was one of the women who organized the International Women's Year in 1975. In the last years of the Russian occupation of Afghanistan, in the late 1980s, she was a UN envoy in Afghanistan working on women's rights. Around 1989, after the Soviet armed forces withdrew by February, she told me that under the Russian occupation in the major urban centers, like Kabul, there had been enormous gains in the rights of women. In Kabul, young women were wearing whatever clothes they wanted; they were going to the university; they had plenty of jobs; literacy had sharply increased. This was largely because the men were out fighting

57

somewhere. There were problems, she said. The problems were the U.S.-backed Mujahideen. The United States picked the most vicious and brutal of them to support, namely the Gulbuddin Hekmatyar group. They would throw acid in the faces of the women who were wearing what they thought were the wrong clothes or something or the other. But apart from that, Rasil Basu said, there were tremendous improvements. Rasil Basu wrote several articles about all this, sent them to the major U.S. media outlets, but these publications did not even answer. She sent them to *Ms.* magazine, the leading feminist journal; no answer. She was finally able to publish them in the Asian press, in *Asia Times*, but not in the United States. Her story was the wrong story. Her story was the Soviets protecting women, while the United States supported the murderous gangsters who throw acid in the faces of women. That's not a story that the U.S. press wanted to publish, however factual. In fact, to this day, I don't think there has been any reporting about these matters. It is just the wrong story, it seems.

Sir Rodric Braithwaite, who wrote the main book in English on the Soviets in Afghanistan (*Afghantsy*, 2012), was the British ambassador to the USSR and then to Russia. During the years of the withdrawal, he followed

58

closely every detail of what was happening. He visited Afghanistan in 2008 and wrote about it in the *Financial Times*, the world's leading business journal, not a communist paper. He just described his impressions of Kabul and reported what people he met told him. He talked to people from all walks of life—pro-government, former Mujahideen, women and men from different social backgrounds. Nostalgia seemed to be the main theme. They looked back fondly at the Soviet period. The person they respected most was Mohammad Najibullah, the last communist head of government.

VIJAY: It is worth pausing here and quoting from the article by Braithwaite, which gives a flavor of the on-the-ground sentiment at that time regarding the U.S.-installed "coalition" government in Kabul:[1]

In Afghanistan today new myths are building up. They bode ill for current western policy. On a recent visit I spoke to Afghan journalists, former Mujahideen, professionals, people working for the "coalition"—natural supporters for its claims to bring peace and reconstruction. They were contemptuous of President Hamid Karzai, whom they compared to Shah Shujah, the British puppet installed during the first

59

Afghan war. Most preferred Mohammad Najibullah, the last communist president, who attempted to reconcile the nation within an Islamic state and was butchered by the Taliban in 1996: DVDs of his speeches are being sold on the streets. Things were, they said, better under the Soviets. Kabul was secure, women were employed, the Soviets built factories, roads, schools and hospitals, Afghan children played safely in the streets. The Russian soldiers fought bravely on the ground like real warriors, instead of killing women and children from the air. Even the Taliban were not so bad: they were good Muslims, kept order, and respected women in their own way. These myths may not reflect historical reality, but they do measure a deep disillusionment with the "coalition" and its policies.

NOAM: Najibullah held out for several years after the Soviet troop withdrawal, despite the Mujahideen attacks. The Afghans in 2008 looked back at him as probably the best person in Afghan history. There were pictures of him everywhere, speeches of his listened to. Braithwaite said he was not sure how much of this is invented in reaction to the current situation, or how much is real. But, he said, it is a reaction to the current situation. I didn't see reports like this in the U.S. press. What Braithwaite said then and what Rasil Basu said then could be brought out today, twenty years later. But it won't be.

VIJAY: Right after 9/11, you began to assemble your book *9/11*. In it you quoted from the French prime minister Hubert Védrine, who said, "If the west goes into Afghanistan, it will be a diabolical trap." After quoting this line in your book, you wrote, "If the United States goes into this war, it'll answer the prayers of Bin Laden and his associates." Could you reflect a little, twenty years later, on Védrine's prophecy and your comment?

NOAM: Bin Laden was quite openly hoping to incite a war between the United States and what's called the Ummah, the Muslim world. He wanted to incite the Muslim world to join him in his effort to overthrow the evil demon, the United States. The best way to do it would be if the United States attacked Muslims, exactly the way it happened in Afghanistan. When the United States invaded the country and the U.S. soldiers arrived in the villages, there were signs of hope. This is what was reported by journalists who were not embedded with the U.S. and NATO troops, who left Kabul for the villages, and who continued to return to these villages over the years. Of

61

course, the Afghans didn't like being invaded. But they saw the United States as a very rich, very powerful country, which maybe would come and help them. That didn't last very long. Now the U.S. invaders of course knew nothing at all about the country, and most of them didn't give a damn about the country. So, they simply turned to local people who could run various regions for them. Who were these local people? They were the warlords who had been terrorizing their own populations for decades. They knew how to run things, they knew the ropes, they offered themselves to the United States as the local chieftains, and the United States was happy to have someone else doing the "nation building." So, who cares if the United States handed over the villages and towns to a bunch of murderers and gangsters? These gangsters immediately instituted their most brutal measures and appointed their mass murderers to run things for them. They figured out a brilliant technique to get rid of their rivals: you just tell the U.S. commander that over in the other village is a guy who supports the Taliban, and the United States will send in the Special Forces to break in at midnight, crash into people's homes, humiliate them, take the men, send them to torture chambers, send them off to Guantánamo. Meanwhile, on the side, send a drone to attack a wedding party and kill a couple dozen people. Pretty soon, you've done the recruitment for the Taliban. Meanwhile, you train the so-called Afghan army with U.S. equipment and U.S. practices. There is massive corruption, with commanders taking money with the claim that they have recruited soldiers who don't exist—the ghost soldiers—and then using that money to feather their nests. Soldiers defect with their equipment. They head for the Taliban.

That's exactly what bin Laden hoped for around the world. Every place the United States attacks, they create more antagonism, more willingness to defend the Muslim world, which is now seen to be under attack for its religious faith. Yes, the response by the United States was almost scripted by bin Laden, and it was a perfect answer to his prayers. The United States didn't care that it was playing along perfectly. Okay, we have a war against the Muslim world, from Afghanistan to Nigeria to the Philippines. After the Battle of Omdurman, when the British defeated the Mahdi in 1898, Hilaire Belloc wrote a famous poem with the line,

Whatever happens, we have got
The Maxim gun, and they have not.

That's basically the imperial slogan. People don't matter. Nothing matters. We have the guns, and we will take control and run it. In the case of Afghanistan after 9/11, the same thing: we can show our muscle and intimidate everyone. The United States had no other interest in Afghanistan.

Let's assess the claim that the United States cares about the Afghan people. Since August 2021, the Taliban have been back in power. They built their bases partly because of the atrocities of the U.S. occupation and war. The only surprise, in my opinion, of their takeover was how they have expanded their array of support. It was a Pashtun organization in 1994 when it was created and during its first term in office between 1996 and 2001. Now, the Taliban have roots in the minority regions, including the Tajik areas of the north. How did they do it? Maybe by buying loyalty or maybe by force, whatever. Either way, they now have that support, and they are the government. But the U.S. government refuses to acknowledge them, despite having negotiated with them for decades. What does this lack of acknowledgment mean? It means that the Afghan government does not have a seat at the United Nations and the Afghan government cannot access its own funds—$9.5 billion—which are in New York banks. The Afghan people are facing a very severe humanitarian crisis, while the United States refuses to release the funds to the Taliban, who are pleading for the funds to be released. The international financial institutions, probably under U.S. pressure, are withholding funds and support. Meanwhile, the international agencies are warning that Afghanistan is facing probably the worst humanitarian crisis in the world, but we must hold on to funds. Why is this so? Because U.S. citizens who were harmed by 9/11 demand reparations from Afghanistan for the death of their family members or for damages. The courts ruled in favor of the 9/11 families. So, President Joe Biden's administration is in a legal bind, although his administration announced it would allow nearly half of the Afghan money to be handed over to the 9/11 families. The U.S. victims of 9/11 claim the funds, and the U.S. court system supports them. How can the United States release the funds to the Afghan government, even as millions of Afghans face starvation? Afghans had nothing to do with 9/11, but they must pay for it. And the United States must show its muscle and intimidate everyone. Is anybody suggesting a court case for Afghans to ask the United States to send them trillions of dollars in reparations for having devastated the country and undermined their society for the past twenty years?

We can run through the atrocities that were carried out in Afghanistan. Are the people of Iraq entitled to start legal cases in the United States to ask for trillions of dollars for the illegal U.S. invasion and destruction of their country, leaving behind misery and ethnic conflict that did not exist before, which is now tearing the region to shreds? Is anybody in the U.S. courts asking for reparations for the Afghans and the Iraqis, or even the people of Honduras or Guatemala or El Salvador or Nicaragua? Untold numbers of Central Americans tortured, their societies devastated, their lives broken. Are there people pressing claims in U.S. courts for them? These questions are unimaginable. Nobody can demand anything from the mafia don, since the don just determines what happens in the world, taking what is needed. If U.S. citizens say, *Starving Afghans paying reparations to us is necessary*, then this is what is going to happen. The courts say, *Yes, that's right*. We're the rulers of the world. We determine what happens. If any of the huge number of victims of U.S. crimes request even an investigation of the crimes, the answer is, *Sorry, the mafia don doesn't do that. That's not the job of the Godfather.* In a nutshell, that's it.

It is not just the United States. It is the imperial attitude. Take France. France was forced to withdraw from its major colony, the source of much of its wealth, Haiti, after the Haitian Revolution of 1804. The French forced the Haitians to pay for their crime of liberating themselves from French rule. The slave owners had to be paid off. Then France imposed a huge indemnity on Haiti, which it didn't pay off until the United States took over the loan after World War II. In 2002, Haiti's president, Jean-Bertrand Aristide, called upon the French to pay $22 billion in reparations. The French said that the issue had been resolved in treaties in the nineteenth century, and that no such reparations would be paid. In 2004, Aristide was overthrown in a coup backed by France and the United States. He was replaced by a military junta, which renounced Haiti's demand for reparations. It was convenient. The French said that they had no responsibility for the situation. There are many examples of the way Britain reacts to these questions, in a way very similar to the French.

There is no disagreement even from liberals in the United States. After the United States had withdrawn from Vietnam, U.S. president Jimmy Carter was asked in March 1977 if the United States owed anything to the people of Southeast Asia for having destroyed Vietnam, Laos, and Cambodia, killed millions of people, devasted the region with chemical warfare, and so on. His answer was quite measured. He said, "We owe them no debt. The destruction was mutual." Okay. That's the liberal president. Reagan was worse: "It was a noble cause, we were right, so they owe us reparations." Or George H. W. Bush: "We're willing to forgive the Vietnamese their crimes against us, because we are a forgiving nation. If they carry out their one responsibility—to find the bones of U.S. pilots who were shot down by the evil North Vietnamese while they were on a mercy mission, flying over North Vietnam in their B-52s to devastate the place, if they do that—and since we are a forgiving country—we will forgive them if they carry out that duty." That's George H. W. Bush, the statesman, not George W. Bush, his son, the maniac. You can go on indefinitely into the annals of imperial history.

VIJAY: In 2015, you told Isabelle Kumar that the United States is the greatest terrorist country in the world. That was the headline. What you were actually talking about was the U.S. assassination campaign by drones in places such as Afghanistan, Pakistan, Somalia, and Yemen. You said that the assassination campaign is the worst terrorist campaign in the world by far, orchestrated in Washington by a liberal democratic administration. The Bureau of Investigative Journalism has a reliable catalogue of the drone strikes. It calculates that between 2010 and 2020, the United States conducted over fourteen thousand drone strikes, killing between 8,858 and 16,901 people (of them 910 to 2,200 were civilians and of them again 283 to 454 were children). Azmat Khan and her colleagues who produced the Civilian Casualty Files on U.S.-led air strikes in Iraq and Syria have found that in half the strikes there was no Islamic State member nearby and the only deaths were of civilians. Between the Bureau— with good information on Afghanistan and Pakistan— and the Civilian Casualty Files—with good information on Iraq and Syria—we have an astounding collection of facts on the murderous nature of these wars. This drone campaign was another recruitment tool for the Taliban in the Afghanistan and Pakistan borderlands, while the air war on Iraq and Syria certainly deepens antipathy to the United States. These are pretty self-evidently terrorist actions.

NOAM: Imagine if Iran were carrying out an international terrorist campaign to assassinate people who it thought might pose a potential danger to Iran? Every leading figure in the U.S. government and the Israeli government, and anybody else who happened to be standing around, would be treated as collateral damage for this campaign. Suppose that they did that. What would the United States say? First of all, we wouldn't say anything, because we'd nuke them and wipe them out. But if we were to say anything, we would say, *They're the greatest terrorist threat in the world.* How can a country dare to go around assassinating people? Which is what the drone campaign is actually all about. It kills people that the United States believes pose a threat to the United States or to its interests. What it actually means is that a couple of guys in northwestern Pakistan are fixing a tire, and a drone circles around them, decides that they are up to no good, and then blasts them with a hellfire missile. That's President Barack Obama's policy. President Donald Trump made it worse, using the Mother of all Bombs on the people of southeastern Afghanistan.

I know that the statement about the United States being a terrorist country is considered an outrageous statement. I make outrageous statements purposely if they are true.

I don't care if they are outrageous. A few years ago, I said that Trump is the most dangerous criminal in world history. How can you be more outrageous than that? But then let's look at the facts. Can you think of any other figure in world history who is as dedicated with passion to destroying the prospects of human life on Earth? Not Hitler, not Genghis Khan, nobody except Trump. The United States had been dragging its feet on efforts to do something about the impending existential catastrophe of environmental destruction. Trump accelerated the devastation. He said, *Who cares? Let's race to the precipice as fast as possible, maximize the use of fossil fuels, including the most dangerous of them, get rid of all the regulations that somewhat mitigate their effect, let's destroy everything as quickly as possible for the benefit of my masters, the people in the ExxonMobil corporate headquarters who need to register their profits tomorrow.* That's the precise order of things. Wipe out everything. Can you find an analogous figure in history? The point is that these are outrageous statements, but they happen to be true, and they are true not just in my opinion. The Gallup organization once made a mistake. This was in 2013, the Obama years, when it asked, "Which country is the greatest threat to world peace?" There was no competitor

71

to the United States. It was far ahead, with Pakistan second, inflated no doubt by the Indian vote. China, North Korea, Israel, and Iran brought up the third tier of threats, far behind the United States. That poll didn't get published in the United States. Look at the key foreign-policy initiatives of the United States government: the invasion and occupation of Afghanistan, the invasion and occupation of Iraq, the blockade of Cuba, the sanctions on Iran and Venezuela—overwhelming opposition from the world's peoples and governments.

After 9/11, President George W. Bush sighed plaintively, Why do they hate us? The point is that we are supposed to be so noble and so wonderful, so why do they hate us? The government did set up a Pentagon investigation to answer Bush's question. Its answer was: *They hate us because of what we have done to them.* That didn't get very far. In 1958, President Dwight D. Eisenhower asked his staff the same question: *Why do they hate us? We've been so good to them. We even forced Israel, Britain, and France to withdraw from the Sinai, not because we opposed it but because they were getting into our turf. We're the only ones who can do things like that. They shouldn't do it. They're the nineteenth-century people. So, we kick them out. And yet, the people are not grateful to us. They still hate us.* Well, there was an answer given by the National Security Council, basically the same one that was given to Bush: *They hate us because of what we do to them.*

Can't imagine why the remnants of Native Americans might have some negative feelings about the United States, or why, say, Mexicans could look at the town where I live in occupied Mexico and say something was wrong with a war of aggression; we stole half of Mexico from Mexico, now the Southwestern and Western United States. How could they have any negative feelings about that? It's all for the benefit of civilization. In fact, if they don't know it already, they could read the leading American writers, people like Ralph Waldo Emerson or Walt Whitman, who asked what a bunch of ignorant Mexicans have to do with the future of the human race? You don't have to read crazed imperial maniacs like Theodore Roosevelt. You can read one of the liberal commentators, like Emerson and Whitman, who were in a more modulated tone saying pretty much the same thing. Apologists for the British Empire said the same: *Look at all the wonderful things we're doing for India after we've destroyed them.*

VIJAY: Yes, that's what they said. And as for their crimes, they have tried their best to bury all memory of them. I remember reading about how the British government hid 1.2 million files in Hanslope Park in London that dealt with the role of Britain in the slave trade, in the Boer War, and in the decolonization process. Thousands of files on the bloody war inflicted by Britain on Kenya in the 1950s have been destroyed. In the margins of a document on Britain's forced labor regime in Kenya, a colonial official wrote, "It must on no account be published." That's the general attitude. Either to hide the actual events of the past and to prevent its being taught or to couch the brutality, as if the railway lines and the ports improved the conditions of the lives of the people who had been colonized.

In 2002, when Bush asked the question of "why do they hate us," you wrote a measured essay on these themes. "Today, Americans do themselves few favors by choosing to believe that 'they hate us' and 'hate our freedoms.' On the contrary," you wrote, "these are people who like Americans and admire much about the U.S., including its freedoms. What they hate is official policies that deny them the freedoms to which they, too, aspire."[2] In 1999, Samuel Huntington wrote in *Foreign Affairs*, "While the U.S. regularly denounces various countries as 'rogue states,' in the eyes of many countries it is becoming the rogue superpower . . . the single greatest external threat to their societies."[3] That was Huntington, the most celebrated mainstream political scientist of his time. That was in 1999, before George W. Bush articulated his national security strategy in 2002, which enshrined the doctrine of preventive war. In August 2003, you described the perils of this doctrine: "The grand strategy authorizes Washington to carry out 'preventive war': *Preventive*, not preemptive. Whatever the justifications for preemptive war might be, they do not hold for preventive war, particularly as that concept is interpreted by its current enthusiasts: the use of military force to eliminate an invented or imagined threat, so that even the term 'preventive' is too charitable. Preventive war is, very simply, the 'supreme crime' condemned at Nuremberg" (*Hegemony or Survival*, 2003).

After 9/11, the Taliban suggested that if the United States provided a dossier with evidence for who committed the crimes, it would consider handing over bin Laden and al-Qaeda to a third country, perhaps Pakistan. This would give the Taliban the ability to say that they did not technically hand over these people to the United States directly. Why did the United States reject this offer? Why did the United States reject Abdul Haq's warning that a war would kill enormous numbers of Afghans? In other words, does the United States act merely to exercise power, or are there other interests of property at work?

NOAM: In the case of Iraq, it was a horrendous crime, an illegal war, as the United Nations conceded in 2004. But at least you can think of a strategic interest. Iraq is one of the world's major oil producers, and that, too, very cheap oil. You don't have to do deep-sea drilling; you just stick a pipe in the ground, and you get the right kind of oil. Iraq is right in the center of the world's major oil-producing region. It is a very good reason for the United States to want to control and dominate it, like Hitler trying to invade the Caucasus to gain control of its oil resources. This is understandable.

In the case of Afghanistan, there's nothing. The United States had no interest in Afghanistan. It was of no strategic interest. There was nothing to gain by it. It was just, *We're angry. We want to show our muscle, intimidate everyone, make sure nobody in the world has any misconceptions about our capacity to use force and violence, and our willingness to do it if you step on our toes. You, the world, better understand that.* That was quite important at that time. Abdul Haq said so just as the bombs began to fall. The world opposed the invasion of Afghanistan. That is now forgotten. The United

States said, *We don't care what you think. We've got the power. We control the means of violence. We do what we want. If we're angry, we will show our muscle and intimidate everyone.* Usually when a great power carries out some military operation, it is for a strategic interest, sometimes not.

Do what you have to do to control the world. The United States is the Godfather, who does not accept successful defiance even from the smallest country. Just like the Godfather: if some small shopkeeper doesn't pay protection money, the Godfather won't even notice the money, but he still sends in the goons to smash up the shop. You don't want people to get the wrong idea. It's like the domino theory: sometimes you don't want the contagion to spread. It's a leading principle of international affairs. One of the most horrifying instances is the U.S. torture of the Haitians, which has been going on since 1804; another is the torture of Cuba, which has been going on since 1959. We should recognize that there is no country in the world that has anything like the capacity of the United States to inflict brutal harm and violence everywhere in the world. Nobody else, for instance, can impose sanctions. When the United States imposes sanctions, they are third-party sanctions that everyone has to live up to no matter how much they hate them. Nobody in the world can come anywhere near this kind of power and violence. That's imperialism.

Why has the United States, for sixty years, continued to insist on torturing Cubans and on trying to destroy a small Caribbean island that offers no military threat? President John F. Kennedy launched a major terrorist war against Cuba, which set the stage for an international confrontation—the missile crisis, that almost led to global destruction—and a blockade that has lasted for sixty years. When the USSR collapsed and Cuba seemed isolated, President Bill Clinton outflanked the Republicans from the right to intensify the blockade and try to crush the Cuban Revolution. This goes right till today, with the whole world opposed to U.S. policy. If you look at the most recent votes in the United Nations, 184 countries say that the United States should end the blockade, while two countries—the United States and Israel—say it should continue.

The whole world obeys U.S. orders, but not all, actually. China does not.

That's the China threat, really. If you look at it, China does not follow U.S. orders. China refuses to be intimidated. That's the great China threat. Cuba is the same.

In fact, one of the good things about the United States is that it is an unusually open society. So, we do have access, to an unusual degree, to internal government planning documents; it is not perfect, but quite a lot is available by comparative standards. So, we know what the Kennedy and Johnson administrations were thinking when they launched a major terrorist war against Cuba, including the blockade. Why launch this? Because of Castro's "successful defiance" of U.S. policy; the term "successful defiance" is from a National Intelligence Estimate done by the CIA in March 1960. This successful defiance goes back 150 years, goes back to the Monroe Doctrine of 1823, which declared the U.S. intention to dominate the hemisphere. The United States could not do it at that time because Britain was much too powerful. U.S. grand planners—such as John Quincy Adams (the intellectual author of Manifest Destiny)—pointed out to his cabinet colleagues in the 1820s that even though they could not conquer Cuba then, because of British power, *over time, British power will decline. Our power will increase. Especially after we exterminate the native population and take over what's called the national territory.* Over time, Adams said, *Cuba will fall into our hands by the laws of political gravitation, the way an apple falls from the tree.* In fact, this happened in 1898 when Cuba was about to liberate itself from Spain, but the United States intervened to prevent the liberation and forced Cuba to become pretty much a U.S. colony until 1959, when Fidel Castro initiated his successful defiance of U.S. demands that had begun 150 years previously.

The United States cannot tolerate defiance, particularly successful defiance. When Maurice Bishop of the New Jewel Movement took control over Grenada and tried to advance a limited social democratic agenda, the United States saw this as defiance. The Carter administration cut funds, imposed restrictions, set up the basis for the invasion conducted by the Reagan administration where six thousand U.S. Special Forces were presented with eight thousand Medals of Honor for overcoming the resistance of forty Cuban construction workers. An immense triumph. Grenada was not going to move toward successful defiance. Britain opposed the U.S. move, but they adhered to it just as they adhere to U.S. sanctions against Cuba. European countries can get up the courage to vote against the United States in the United Nations, but they obey the U.S. sanctions; this is the case with Iran, where most European states are strongly opposed to the U.S. sanctions on Iran, but they obey them; they don't step on the toes of the Godfather. If you do, you'll be punished. Europe has some reserves to defy the United States, but they don't do it. They could be thrown out of the international financial system, which the United States runs. But it would take a little bit of courage and a little bit of independence to defy the United States. It is way too much to expect of European leaders. So, they just tag along, follow the orders of the Godfather, even when they oppose them.

There's an ugly pattern. Israel carries out periodic, murderous, destructive attacks with U.S. weapons and U.S. support against the Palestinians, most brutally in Gaza. If they run out of weapons, which happens regularly, the Israelis turn to the United States to replenish them, which the United States can do just by transferring weapons that it stores in Israel. Israel calls these attacks, politely, mowing the lawn. In August 2021, in the West Bank in the Jordan Valley, which the United States and the Israelis have basically taken over and kicked out the Palestinians from, Israeli army troops entered a remote village and destroyed a solar panel system that had been set up by an Italian humanitarian organization. The Israeli newspaper *Haaretz*, in an editorial, said, "A great deal of sadism is required to leave dozens of people, including the elderly and children, without electricity in the summer heat of the Jordan Valley."[4] It's illegal, the Israeli soldiers said, destroy it. Then the Europeans will return and likely rebuild it. Same thing: follow the Godfather's orders, maybe do bits and pieces to repair the damage, but basically go along with the mafia imperialism.

The British did the same thing with the destruction and deindustrialization of the richest country in the world, India. It was a massive robbery to enrich Britain. The British ran the world's greatest narco-trafficking operation to force China, through the opium trade, to submit to British commercial practices and accept British goods that they did not want. When the Chinese said no, then they had to be destroyed with gunboats. The Summer Palace was destroyed and whatever could be stolen was stolen, including Hong Kong. That's imperial violence. The United States is acting in the same way as Britain did and as France did and as Germany and Italy did in their smaller domains, with major genocides in Africa. That's the way great powers have always operated.

VIJAY: There's some drama around a bust of Winston Churchill that goes in and out of the Oval Office in the White House. It is notable that the U.S. ruling class has this fantasy about Churchill. A young Churchill went to

India to fight in "a lot of jolly little wars against barbarous peoples." In the Swat Valley, in today's Pakistan, Churchill and his troops mowed down local resistance with extreme violence. When he reflected on that murderous war, he wrote that his troops had to be bloody because the people of Swat had a "strong aboriginal propensity to kill." There is a direct line between the real Churchill and the people who keep his bust on their desks.

In 1993, you wrote an article in *Z Magazine*, which discussed the idea of the "Pentagon system." Two concepts played a role in this assessment. One of them was the idea of the military–industrial complex, a term associated with Eisenhower's farewell speech ("Eisenhower knew about this very well," you told me a few years ago, "because he had fostered it for eight years"). The other is the idea of military Keynesianism. Competition between various capitalists leads to great instability in the economy, with the competitive pressure resulting in regular business downturns; during these downturns, governments are called upon to increase spending to bail out the forsaken capitalists—this is the basic architecture of Keynesianism. In the United States, deathly fear of socialism led to the salvage funds of Keynesianism going toward the military rather than the social sector. This is military Keynesianism. Here's your explanation from 1993:

NOAM: Like all advanced societies, the United States has relied on state intervention in the economy from its origins, though for ideological reasons, the fact is commonly denied. During the post–World War II period, such "industrial policy" was masked by the Pentagon system, including the Department of Energy (which produces nuclear weapons) and NASA, converted by the Kennedy administration to a significant component of the state-directed public subsidy to advanced industry. By the late 1940s, it was taken for granted in government–corporate circles that the state would have to intervene massively to maintain the private economy. In 1948, with postwar pent-up consumer demand exhausted and the economy sinking back into recession, Truman's "cold-war spending" was regarded by the business press as a "magic formula for almost endless good times" (*Steel*), a way to "maintain a generally upward tone" (*Business Week*). The *Magazine of Wall Street* saw military spending as a way to "inject new strength into the entire economy," and a few years later, found it "obvious that foreign economies as well as our own are now mainly dependent on the scope of continued arms spending in this country," referring to the international military Keynesianism that finally succeeded in reconstructing state capitalist industrial societies abroad and laying the basis for the huge expansion of Transnational Corporations (TNCs), at that time mainly U.S. based.

The Pentagon system was considered ideal for these purposes. It imposes on the public a large burden of the costs (research and development, R&D) and provides a guaranteed market for excess production, a useful cushion for management decisions. Furthermore, this form of industrial policy does not have the undesirable side effects of social spending directed to human needs. Apart from unwelcome redistributive effects, the latter policies tend to interfere with managerial prerogatives; useful production may undercut private gain, while state-subsidized waste production (arms, man-on-the-moon extravaganzas, etc.) is a gift to the owner and manager, who will, furthermore, be granted control of any marketable spin-offs. Furthermore, social spending may well arouse public interest and participation, thus enhancing the threat of democracy; the public cares about hospitals, roads, neighborhoods, and so on, but has no opinion about the choice of missiles and high-tech fighter planes.

The defects of social spending do not taint the military Keynesian alternative, which had the added advantage that it was well adapted to the needs of advanced industry: computers and electronics generally, aviation, and a wide range of related technologies and enterprises. The Pentagon system of course served other purposes. As global enforcer, the U.S. needs intervention forces, and an intimidating posture to facilitate their use. But its economic role has always been central, a fact well known to military planners. Army Plans Chief General James Gavin, in charge of army R&D under Eisenhower, noted that "what appears to be intense interservice rivalry in most cases . . . is fundamentally industrial rivalry." It was also recognized from the outset that these goals require "sacrifice and discipline" on the part of the general public (National Security Council, policy paper 68). It was therefore necessary, Secretary of State Dean Acheson urged, "to bludgeon the mass mind" of Congress and recalcitrant officials with the communist threat in a manner "clearer than truth," and to "scare the hell out of the American people," as Senator Arthur Vandenberg interpreted the message. To carry out these tasks has been a prime responsibility of intellectuals throughout these years.

VIJAY: The Stockholm International Peace Research Institute (SIPRI) maintains detailed records of military spending based on what governments declare in their budgets. In 2021, SIPRI's report showed that in 2020 the United States spent an estimated $778 billion on its military, an increase of 4.4 percent over 2019. Based on what you just said, this is not an accurate assessment of the total military spending, since it does not include the full amounts tucked into other budgets (Department of Energy, NASA, and various intelligence agencies). Nonetheless, even without these additional amounts in the total, the United States accounts for 39 percent of total military expenditure in 2020. That is, the United States. with 4.25 percent of the world's population, accounts for almost 40 percent of the world's military expenditure. The United States can destroy any country in the world. And yet, it seems to consistently be defeated by the world's peasant armies (Vietnam, Afghanistan).

None of these facts—and they are facts that are culled from respectable publications—frame the stories in the major newspapers and for the major television channels and web-based publications. That was the theme of your classic book, written with Edward Herman, on the suffocation of the news industry—*Manufacturing Consent:*

The Political Economy of the Mass Media (1988)—and the previous book that you both wrote together, *Counter-Revolutionary Violence: Bloodbaths in Fact and Propaganda* (1973). The history of the previous book, little known these days, is that after it was advertised by Warner Modular Publications, the head of the book division of Warner Publishing tried to suppress it, then simply had the firm destroy all remaining copies of the book, and then put the entire publisher out of business as punishment for trying to distribute it. What annoyed Warner Publishing is that the book had carefully dissected the public record over the terrors of U.S. action in Vietnam, Indonesia, Bangladesh, and elsewhere. It was, the head of Warner said, "a scurrilous attack on respected Americans."

In the preface, Richard Falk suggests that the term *mafia*—which you have used—is "characteristic of government operations." The actions of the U.S. government, in places such as Vietnam and Thailand, are like those of the mafia, you contend; but what makes it difficult to establish in popular discourse is the screen provided by the mass media, which operates more and more like a Ministry of Propaganda than a normal news operation. Reports of massacres do make it into the media, but

88

routinely these are the massacres done by the enemies of the United States rather than the massacres conducted by United States personnel. It is always the enemy of the United States that is said to conduct a massacre, but never the United States or its close allies. It is fundamental to U.S. propaganda to ensure that the United States is seen as benevolent. Here you are with Edward Herman from your (essentially proscribed) 1973 book:

The regularly publicized and condemned bloodbaths, whose victims are worthy of serious concern, often turn out, upon close examination, to be fictional in whole or in part. These mythical or semi-mythical bloodbaths have served an extremely important public relations function in mobilizing support for American military intervention in other countries. This has been particularly true in the case of Vietnam. Public opinion has tended to be negative, and the warmakers have had to strain mightily to keep the American people in line. The repeated resort to fabrication points up the propagandistic role that the "bloodbath" has played in Washington's devoted attention to this subject. The evidence on myth creation also makes obvious the fact that stories emanating from this source, whether produced by the military, intelligence, or state-affiliated "scholarship," should be

89

evaluated by the standards and methods normally employed
in assessing the output of any Ministry of Propaganda.

The drone program is unpopular and seemingly inefficient. This is the same with sanctions and the blockade against Cuba. Yet, despite opposition of one kind or another, the public mood in the United States seems to be that these kinds of policies should continue.

NOAM: First of all, the overwhelming opposition to the drone program is international. I haven't seen the question raised in polls, but I suspect that if you asked people in the United States, *is it okay to have*—they would never use the word *blockade—sanctions on Cuba*, probably the answer will be *yes*.

You can read op-eds in the *New York Times*. One in August 2021 was by two specialists on Cuba.[5] They said, essentially, *All this talk about a sanctions blockade is nonsense. The United States provides humanitarian aid to Cuba, provides food aid, and so on.* They even made the mistake of giving a reference, a hyperlink. Well, I took the trouble of looking up the reference. It was to a U.S. government publication that says the opposite of what they claim. It says, *The US does not allow humanitarian aid to Cuba.* I had assumed that the *New York Times* had fact-checked such articles, looked up these sorts of references, noticed that it says the opposite in each case, and so on. Obviously, I'm wrong. They don't. This is pretty normal, I should say. There are things you just don't look at because they are so obviously true or false. You get this kind of thing in the so-called leftist journals as well. Take the *New York Review of Books*, which is a critical journal, where you could find critical articles on U.S. policy. In the journal, you had Russell Baker, a good, honest, leftist critic, reviewing Edmund Morgan's collection of essays on U.S. history.[6] Baker was amazed at what he learned, which was that when the colonialists came to the Western Hemisphere, there was almost nobody here; from the boiling tropics to the frozen north there were about a million people straggling around. He was off by about 80 million. They weren't just straggling around, they had advanced civilizations. That's the *New York Review of Books.* I checked over the course of the next few months if there would be a letter about it, but nothing. They must have heard some objections, because about four months later there was a small correction. They said that there was a mistake in the numbers. They misquoted what he had said, saying that he was referring merely to North

America, and that it was not one million, but 18 million. Okay. Slight improvement. But barely; I mean, it's nothing.

At the end of the war on Vietnam, a couple of years afterward, there was a media study group at the University of Massachusetts–Amherst that did a study of attitudes of UMASS students. This is UMASS–Amherst, an advanced college with the best students. One of the questions asked to the students was could you estimate the number of Vietnamese killed in the war. Their mean estimate was 100,000. The official number is 2 million. The actual number is probably 4 million. Their estimate was 100,000. Suppose you took a poll in Germany and young people from the most advanced educational institutions were asked about the death toll in the Holocaust, what would you get? Suppose they said, 200,000. We'd think that there is a problem in Germany. Do we think that there is a problem in the United States? Can't be. The United States does not have problems. It's like our wars. Take the invasion of Iraq again. Can you find anyone in high places, major commentators in the media, who says that the invasion was a crime? What they might say is that it was a blunder. Obama is praised because he said it was a "strategic blunder." He echoed Nazi generals, who said that invading the USSR was a "strategic blunder" since they felt that they should have knocked out Britain first. Do we praise them as great moral leaders? Not exactly.

There is a concept in U.S. ideology called American exceptionalism. It says that the United States is unique in its benevolence. There are two things wrong with this idea. First is the actual historical record, which is one of violence and savagery. The other is this idea that exceptionalism is unique to the United States. All the previous imperial centers—from Britain to France to the Dutch— had this combination of acts of violence and a self-image of benevolence.

VIJAY: On a television show in 2010, you were asked what you thought about the concept of American exceptionalism. Your answer was very clear, so here it is:

NOAM: Well, first of all, it's not that I'm not a fan of American exceptionalism. That's like saying I'm not a fan of the moon being made out of green cheese. It doesn't exist. Powerful states have quite typically considered themselves to be exceptionally magnificent, and the United States is no exception to that. The basis for it is not very substantial, to put it politely. The problems with American foreign policy are rooted in its essential nature, which we know about. Or we can know about it if we want to. So, you go back to, say, World War II. That's the point at which the United States became a global power. Before that it had conquered the national territory, pretty much exterminated the population, conquered half of Mexico, pretty much taken control over the Western Hemisphere, invaded the Philippines, killed a couple of hundred thousand people. But the real global power up to that time was Britain and others. The United States was not a global power. But it became so after the World War II. And planners met and carefully laid out plans—they're perfectly public—for how they would run the postwar world. The basic idea was that there should be what they called a Grand Area, which would be completely under U.S. control and within which the United States would not tolerate any expression of sovereignty that interfered with U.S. global designs. There would be no competitor permitted, of course, to the United States. And that area was pretty expansive. It included the Western Hemisphere, East Asia, the former British Empire, which the United States would take over— that includes crucially the Middle East energy reserves, which are the main ones in the world. And top planners pointed out that if we can control Middle East oil, we can control the world. And then of course it included as much of Eurasia as possible, at least its commercial and industrial center, Western Europe. That was the Grand Area. And within that Grand Area the United States would dominate and limit the exercise of sovereignty. Well, of course, to a large extent that policy was implemented in the following years. Of course, it was too ambitious, the system of power eroded, there was decolonization, which weakened authority, other industrial powers reconstituted themselves from the war. By around 1970 the world was basically tri-polar economically: a U.S.-based North America, a mostly German-based Europe, and at that time a Japan-based Asia were major economic powers. And since then, it's fragmented even more. Nevertheless, this essential policy remains, and that's why we have maybe eight hundred military bases around the world—nobody else does. Why, we spend about as much on the military as the rest of the world combined and are technologically far more advanced with means of destruction on the planning table to go beyond anything anyone has dreamt of; and why, we've spent a couple of trillion dollars invading a couple of countries in the Middle East and Central Asia and still occupying them and on and on. Those are very serious problems.

VIJAY: That pretty much sums up the nature of U.S. imperialism. One reason why there might be this lack of knowledge about the imperialist dynamic of U.S. policy is the distance between the cultural world in the United States and the worlds where the U.S. wars take place. In the *New York Review of Books*, in your 1975 article on the U.S. withdrawal, you wrote, "The U.S. government was defeated in Indochina, but only bruised at home." I found that phrase evocative, *only bruised at home.* The U.S. government withdrew from Afghanistan on August 15, 2021, but it doesn't even seem to be bruised at home. It seems to have made no impact.

NOAM: Well, in Indochina, seventy thousand U.S. soldiers were killed and there was a huge protest movement at the very end of the war. Very different from Afghanistan, because for the people of the United States, Afghanistan was an easy war. The fighting was done by a professional army, often Special Forces, not by draftees. The U.S. casualties were grave, but not as serious as in Indochina. The war was a relative sideshow. The United States had basically no interest in it. Couldn't figure out an easy way to get out, but had no strategic interest. Though the columnists talked about how this was a huge defeat, about how the American Century was over and so on, for most people in the United States it was a shrug of the shoulders. It had basically no effect on U.S. power. It is one of those rare wars of aggression that had no geostrategic purpose and where the troops were pulled out to be transferred elsewhere. Barely bruised at home, with some reputations harmed.

VIJAY: If the United States had been able to occupy Afghanistan and convert it into a client state, there are three advantages that it might have enjoyed. First, in 2010, a U.S. military report estimated that there was at least $1 trillion worth of precious metals in Afghanistan. Later that year, Afghanistan's minister of mines, Wahidullah Shahrani, said that the actual number could have been three times as much. There is no need to directly colonize a country to exploit its wealth, as we can see from other parts of the world, but nonetheless it is important to put that on the table. Second, if the United States had been able to control Afghanistan, it could have prevented the full flowering of the Chinese-led Belt and Road Initiative, which aims to build infrastructure across Central Asia, including Afghanistan. Hillary Clinton had hoped to use the United States to build a New Silk Road—as

she described it at a speech in Chennai, India, in 2011—
that would run from India to the Central Asian states, in
order to undermine both Chinese east–west commercial
developments and Russia's historical links to the Central
Asian states. Third, access to military bases in a clientelist
Afghanistan could have afforded the United States the
opportunity to do its mischief in both China's Xinjiang
Uygur Autonomous Region and Iran's eastern provinces.
It is true the withdrawal had no effect on U.S. power, but
if the United States had been able to create a client state it
might have enhanced U.S. power in Asia, in particular for
its heightened contest against China and Russia.

3
Iraq

VIJAY: In the first week of December 2021, just a few weeks after the United States was forced to withdraw from Afghanistan, the U.S. military announced that it was going to alter its profile in Iraq. No longer was the U.S. military on a combat mission in that country; it would now merely "advise, assist, and enable" Iraqi forces as they fought the Islamic State (ISIS). The United States moved its logistical headquarters from Anbar Province, Iraq, to Kuwait. But this withdrawal marked merely another milestone in a long-term departure from Iraq that began in 2007. That year, the U.S. government failed to get a new Status of Forces Agreement from the Iraqi parliament, which would have afforded U.S. troops, among other things, extra-territorial protection while they served in Iraq; in other words, U.S. troops did not want to operate under the mandate of either Iraqi law or the Iraqi lawmakers, who insisted on exercising their sovereignty over their country. None of this applies to the northern part of Iraq, the Kurdish autonomous regions, which the United States carved out of Iraq in 1991. The determinate reason why the United States had to conduct this steady withdrawal from Iraq in 2007 and then again in 2021 is that the various Iraqi governments, from the 2005 government of Ibrahim al-Jaafari (Islamic Dawa Party) to the current parliament dominated by Muqtada al-Sadr, would not tolerate a permanent U.S. military presence in Iraq. Despite the normal tensions between Iran and Iraq, there is little disagreement that Iran—rather than the United States—benefited from the removal of its adversary Saddam Hussein. Within the space of two years, between 2001 and 2003, the United States used its military force to remove two of Iran's great adversaries, the Taliban in Afghanistan and Saddam Hussein in Iraq. These wars provided Iran with a great strategic advantage. Was this possibility not discussed by the backroom boys in Washington?

NOAM: No need for the backroom. It was public. The neoconservative movement—Project for a New American Century (PNAC), with Donald Rumsfeld and Paul Wolfowitz—had a plan, which was public, to use American power to expand its control over the region. I think 9/11 was a welcome pretext for them. Right after 9/11, Rumsfeld's notes show that these men felt that they had a chance to do a range of things.

VIJAY: On the afternoon of September 11, 2001, Rumsfeld gathered his team and gave them his thoughts, which were jotted down by Stephen Cambone, one of Rumsfeld's advisors. Cambone's notes are reflective of the thinking of the men of PNAC and of the neoconservatives in the Bush administration:

Hard to get good case. Need to move swiftly. Near term target needs—go massive—sweep it all up, things related and not. Best info fast. Judge whether good enough [to] hit SH [Saddam Hussein] at the same time—not only UBL [Osama bin Laden]. Tasks Jim Haynes [Pentagon lawyer] to talk with PW [Paul Wolfowitz] for additional support. . . . connection with UBL.

The desire to attack Saddam Hussein was right there in Cambone's notes of Rumsfeld's comments at 2:40 p.m., just hours after the Pentagon had been struck at 9:37 a.m. Evidence was unnecessary. A great desire to attack Iraq was evident.

PNAC has an interesting history. The phrase "American Century" comes from the publisher of *Life*, Henry Luce, who wanted to indicate in the 1940s that the United States would be the leading power at least for the century before it. The defeat in Vietnam created what was known as "Vietnam Syndrome," the sense that the United

States no longer wanted to bear the awful responsibility of being the world's leading power. These neoconservatives were keen to overcome what they considered the post–Vietnam era drift. A set of influential Washington intellectuals and policy analysts who went in and out of government formed part of Team B, a policy group put together in the U.S. Defense Department in 1990 during the George H. W. Bush administration. Dick Cheney led the team, eager to prevent the collapse of the USSR causing a "peace dividend." Their Defense Planning Guidance of 1992 noted, "Our first objective is to prevent the re-emergence of a new rival, either on the territory of the former Soviet Union or elsewhere, that poses a threat on the order of that posed by the Soviet Union. This is the dominant consideration and requires that we endeavor to prevent any hostile power from dominating a region whose resources would, under consolidated control, be sufficient to generate global power. Our strategy must now refocus on precluding the emergence of any potential future global competitor." During the Clinton years, this group of neoconservatives created PNAC. Their report from 2000—*Rebuilding America's Defenses*—argued that if "American peace is to be maintained and expanded," then this Pax Americana "must have a secure foun-

dation on unquestioned U.S. military pre-eminence."
Before 9/11, George W. Bush started the massive expansion of U.S. military capacity, which was extended after 9/11. His 2002 National Security Strategy reads a lot like a PNAC manual, largely because it was written by these men. Here is a familiar sentence, for example: "Our forces should be strong enough to dissuade potential adversaries from pursuing a military build-up in the hopes of surpassing, or equaling, the power of the United States."

Cambone's cryptic notes of Rumsfeld's statements are indicative of this kind of thinking: *go massive, sweep it all up, things related and not.* Iraq was in the crosshairs from the start.

NOAM: To really understand Iraq, you have to go back to 1979. That's when U.S. policies toward Iraq sharply changed to strong support for Saddam Hussein, which mainly had to do with Iran. As soon as the Iranian Revolution took place in 1979 and the Islamic Republic asserted itself, the Carter administration ordered General Robert Huyser to stir up a military uprising, to overthrow the new government, to restore the shah of Iran or some such dictator, but they could not manage it. Carter's national security advisor, Zbigniew Brzezinski, was quite open about this, as was the last de facto Israeli ambassador in Tehran, Uri Lubrani, who was even more extreme, saying, *If you are willing to kill ten thousand people in the streets, you could restore the shah.* . . . After Iraq invaded Iran in 1980, the United States immediately turned to strong support for Iraq. There is a famous photograph of Donald Rumsfeld shaking hands with Saddam Hussein, making deals to send weapons to try to support Iraq's unprovoked invasion of Iran, which was a brutal, murderous invasion that resulted in the death of hundreds of thousands of Iranians. The Iraqi army used chemical weapons against the Iranians and against the Iraqi Kurds, even against the Iraqis themselves; the weapons came from the West. Ronald Reagan himself denied that this happened. They blamed it on Iran, although Iran did not do any of these atrocities. Reagan intervened to block any congressional statement that opposed the use of the chemical weapons against the Kurds. Later, this was brought up as one of the reasons to overthrow Saddam Hussein. But, in fact, the love affair between the United States and Saddam was so extreme that Saddam received a gift that no country other than Israel could receive, which was the allowance to attack a U.S. warship and face no retaliation.

VIJAY: You are referring to two events that are simply not part of the common knowledge of people who otherwise are well informed. Iraq's army shot at a U.S. warship? So did Israel's, and there was no retaliation? How is it possible that these incidents are so poorly known? On June 8, 1967, Israeli fighter jets and torpedo boats fired at the USS *Liberty*, which was in international waters, during the Six-Day War. The attack killed thirty-four crew members. Israel apologized, and that was that. Twenty years later, on May 17, 1987, Iraqi jets fired two Exocet missiles at the USS *Stark*, killing thirty-seven crew members, with nothing more than an apology afterward. Israel paid modest compensation for the lives of the lost servicemen ($6.89 million in 1968–1969), namely $1.4 million per person in 2020 dollars; the families of the 9/11 victims will receive $3.1 million per person in 2020 dollars from the seized Afghan external reserves. Iraq only paid compensation in 2011, when the U.S.-imposed government agreed to disburse $400 million for the 1987 attack on the USS *Stark* and for prisoners of war and others in the subsequent years. Post–U.S. occupation Afghanistan and Iraq have had to pay far more for these attacks than Israel did, a point to be noted in this discussion. But, of course, these two U.S. ships were military vessels. The

United States has—as you have pointed out a number of times, Noam—fired at civilian vessels, including an Iranian aircraft.

NOAM: That's right. The United States intervened directly in the war that Iraq fought against Iran. On July 3, 1988, the USS *Vincennes* fired guided missiles at Iran Air Flight 655 from Tehran to Dubai in a clearly identified commercial corridor, killing all 290 civilians on board. The U.S. ship went back to port in Norfolk, Virginia, and was given a rousing welcome. The captain, Will Rogers, was given a medal by George H. W. Bush. It was in this context that Bush said that Americans never apologize for anything that they do. You want to shoot down a commercial airliner, fine. We give you a Medal of Honor. Iran realized that it cannot fight the United States, and they accepted a settlement, a capitulation. It was probably at this time that Iran initiated a small program of nuclear weapons, probably to balance out the U.S. attempt to create a nuclear weapons program in Iraq. George Bush invited Iraqi nuclear engineers to the United States to receive advanced training in nuclear weapons production at that point, which was a severe threat to Iran.

In April 1990, Bush sent a delegation to Iraq to convey his good wishes to Saddam. It was led by Republican senator—and Senate majority leader—Bob Dole. They praised Saddam for his great achievements and said that Saddam should disregard all the critical comments in the American press. Senator Alan Simpson of Wyoming told Saddam that his problem was not with the U.S. government but with the U.S. press. *We have this crazy First Amendment business, so the government cannot properly shut down the press, but it is best to ignore it.* Dole said that the one commentator at *Voice of America* who had been critical of Saddam was removed. They told Saddam that they were doing what they could to end this unfair criticism of Bush's friend. Over the objections of the U.S. Treasury Department, major shipments of agricultural material were to be sent over; this was material for the rejuvenation of agriculture in areas wiped out by Saddam's use of the Western chemical weapons against the Kurds.

A couple of months later, Saddam made a mistake. He disobeyed orders and invaded Kuwait, apparently thinking that he had a green light. The U.S. ambassador to Iraq, April Glaspie, had delivered a sort of ambiguous statement, which Saddam thought was a green light to invade. He quickly discovered that he had made a mistake and offered to withdraw. The United States wasn't willing to accept the withdrawal. The United States desperately wanted the war. Saddam offered successive proposals over the next nine months for a kind of political settlement. The United States didn't even respond. Leaks came from the U.S. State Department, but the press refused to report them. One paper did report it, a tabloid in Long Island; leakers were sending bits and pieces to the Long Island suburban paper when the *New York Times* refused to run them. Later, Thomas Friedman did mention it, but barely, saying something like, *There are these rumors about Saddam's proposals, but the State Department is disputing that.* So it went, all the way to the days of the U.S. invasion, which could easily have been avoided and which was deeply unpopular. There were all kinds of fabricated stories about babies being thrown out of incubators and Saddam's threats to invade Saudi Arabia, all exposed later. But they were useful for stirring up the U.S. population; the United States was about the only country where there was any support for the bombing of Iraq.

VIJAY: Saddam Hussein's troops entered Kuwait on August 2, 1990. Ten days later, on August 12, and then again on August 23, Saddam Hussein offered to withdraw from

Kuwait. Ten days into his occupation of Kuwait, Saddam told Iraqi radio that he would withdraw if the Israelis withdrew from "occupied Arab land"; since this was simply not going to happen, the offer of a withdrawal was merely rhetorical. You are not referring to this first offer. You are referring to the offer of August 23, when the Iraqis sent a secret démarche to the White House. This is what had been reported in Long Island's *Newsday*.[1] What Saddam wanted was "sole control" of the Rumaila oil field, which the Iraqis accused the Kuwaitis of drilling into laterally, as well as "guaranteed access" to the Persian Gulf. This was neither accepted nor reported beyond *Newsday*. As the months dragged on, Saddam's demands weakened. By January 1991, he wanted almost nothing; he was happy to withdraw his troops with some dignity. This time, the *New York Times* carried the story on page 8, which was driven by the fact that Yasir Arafat of the Palestine Liberation Organization had carried a message to the United States for a dial-down of tensions.[2] That article mentioned the previous offers from Saddam and then admitted that the Iraqis were willing to withdraw for almost nothing: "Some Iraqi officials have hinted that Mr. Hussein would be willing to withdraw from Kuwait after winning some statement from the Administration that it intends to place

111

the Palestinian problem higher on its agenda." Even this was unacceptable. As you said, the United States wanted the war. The effective surrender of Saddam Hussein was not only barely reported at the time, but it is also now almost universally forgotten. The general narrative is that the United States stood firm against a recalcitrant Saddam Hussein and forced him to leave Kuwait. This allows the United States to claim that the war of 1991 was a heroic war.

NOAM: Correct. The invasion by the United States was regarded as a great, heroic achievement. The U.S. army succeeded in overcoming the enormous Iraqi army in a very brutal fashion. The harshness of the war was reported mostly in Long Island's *Newsday*, which appears on New York newsstands, to the point where the United States was just using bulldozers to bulldoze Iraqi soldiers, mostly drafted peasants, to bulldoze them as the army moved forward over the earth that covered these Iraqi peasant soldiers, buried in the sand and mud. Meanwhile, the United States bombed everywhere they could, the infrastructure of Iraq devastated beyond imagination. George H. W. Bush explained what was happening clearly, *We've shown that what we say goes. That's it.* It is sort

112

of like the war on Afghanistan, the muscle intimidating everyone. We didn't want negotiations, even surrender. We wanted a devastating attack to show the world that what we say goes.

The war did not end with the bombing. It was followed up by a harsh sanctions regime put in place by Bill Clinton, although technically these were United Nations sanctions. The UN diplomats were tasked with supervising the oil-for-food program, which allowed Iraq to sell oil and receive food and other things. This was the so-called humane part of the sanctions regime. Both the main UN diplomats—Denis Halliday and Hans von Sponeck—resigned in protest, charging that the sanctions regime was genocidal. Von Sponeck wrote an important book—*A Different Kind of War: The UN Sanctions Regime in Iraq* (2006)—in which he detailed what was going on. Von Sponeck knew more about Iraq at that time than any other Westerner. His staff went about the country collecting information on the severe sadism of the sanctions, and then he laid it out in great detail in his book. The sanctions devastated the population and, as usual, supported the dictator by undermining any possible opposition to him. Saddam had a very efficient food-distribution system that had been recognized by the West.

The people starving under the sanctions flocked under his umbrella for support. The kind of opposition that had overthrown a series of dictators, a popular opposition, could not take place here; Marcos, Suharto, Duvalier, all of them had been overthrown in this period by popular opposition, but this was not possible under the sanctions regime in Iraq, which totally undermined any effort on the part of the population and strengthened Saddam. It is the usual effect of sanctions, incidentally. Von Sponeck's book was basically suppressed. I don't think there was a single review of the book in the United States. There were barely any events that featured him, one of them a small seminar at MIT. His views did not find a wider audience. By 2001, the Iraqi people struggled to survive with dignity.

The United States continued to bomb Iraq through the 1990s, almost as if the United States wanted to let the Iraqis know that the war of 1991 had not ended. When the opportunity came for the United States to invade Iraq, it took it. That invasion of 2003 was against overwhelming public opinion around the world, except in the United States and Israel. In France and Germany, the public was overwhelmingly against the U.S. war, which is why the governments were forced to speak against the war. Thomas Friedman wrote an article in the *New York Times* to say that France should be thrown out of the United Nations Security Council[3]; he said it in the way that children speak in kindergartens: if you don't play by our rules, then leave. The U.S. Senate banned *french* fries in their cafeteria; they renamed them freedom fries. We'll show those French for daring to follow public opinion! Donald Rumsfeld made a very interesting speech in which he distinguished between Old Europe and New Europe. Old Europe is made up of countries like France and Germany, where they follow overwhelming public opinion and opposed the U.S. invasion; New Europe is made up of a bunch of leaders who did support the U.S. invasion over the overwhelming opposition of their populations. Many press reports about the wonders of New Europe appeared, suppressing the fact that although their rulers did support the United States, their populations opposed the war. The most dramatic case was Spain, where Prime Minister José Maria Aznar supported the U.S. invasion, and who was invited to the Azores with Bush and British prime minister Tony Blair to announce it. Aznar was greatly praised in the U.S. press, which failed to mention that about 98 percent of the Spanish people opposed the war. That's a minor thing. New Europe was those rulers who opposed the overwhelming will of their populations. Old Europe, the kind we forget about and want to kick out of the UN Security Council, as Thomas Friedman suggested, was those who actually followed the opinion of their public.

Then comes the war. Humanitarian organizations, just as they did with Afghanistan, warned that the war would create a humanitarian crisis and that the Iraqis could not cope with a major invasion. They anticipated that hundreds of thousands of people would die, which turned out to be an underestimate. It didn't matter. Just as with Afghanistan, we do what we like, we show our muscles. In the case of Iraq, unlike Afghanistan, there was a real strategic purpose: the oil. The invasion was brutal, some of the incidents—such as during the second attack on Fallujah in November 2004—truly shocking. Women and children were allowed to leave, but men had to remain in the city. Then came a major attack by the U.S. Marines, which was lauded in the press. I remember the first day of the attack, when the U.S. forces took over the general hospital, which is a major war crime. The soldiers threw patients on the floor, threw doctors on the floor, and tied them up. The press was euphoric; the *New York Times* had a picture of the general hospital, talking about

116

how wonderful it was and blaming the attack on the "terrorists."[4] The press described how the U.S. Marines found the "packrats" in their "warrens" and killed them. Nobody knows how many people were killed, since we don't count our atrocities. Dangerous weapons were used, including lots of depleted uranium, lots of radioactivity, which increased the rates of cancer. Studies from Iraqi doctors followed, and from Iraqi human rights groups; both showed the scale of the atrocity. The worst crime was that the invasion stirred up ethnic conflict. Before the U.S. invasion, the Shia and Sunni communities lived together, treating each other like two Protestant sects in the United States. They intermarried, they lived in the same neighborhoods, and they often did not know who was whom. A couple of years into the U.S. occupation, they were at war against each other. This ethnic or sectarian war spread all over the Middle East, tearing the entire region to shreds.

In Iraq, the United States could not establish a government pliable enough to run it for them. That became a problem when the United States was forced to withdraw under Iraqi pressure in 2007. The Bush administration produced a Status of Forces Agreement (SOFA) in November 2007, which they wanted the Iraqi government to accept. For the first time, this SOFA stated explicitly the U.S. motives for their war. Anybody with their eyes open knew it already, but this was an explicit statement. The agreement provided special privileges to U.S. corporations, meaning U.S. energy corporations, to exploit Iraqi resources. That was one point. The second was that the United States had to have permanent military bases in Iraq. These are the two essential points of the SOFA. To make sure that everyone understood that the U.S. government was not going to budge from these points, in January 2008, when the U.S. president presented the budget, he put out signing statements to say that he would ignore anything that interfered with the proposals in the SOFA agreement. This was really serious, which meant that the United States was going to insist on giving special privileges to U.S. corporations and to the existence of permanent military bases. The press cooperated by never reporting it, and commentators and scholars did not report it. It was the most important statement about the war.

We know about the pretext. The first pretext was what Tony Blair called the "single question" for the invasion: will Saddam end his nuclear weapons program? They couldn't find any evidence for such weapons or any other weapons of mass destruction. Before the war on Iraq,

Rumsfeld and Dick Cheney started their torture program to find out if they could conjure up a relationship between Saddam and al-Qaeda, which is completely ludicrous since they were enemies, but they tried to find some evidence, which would have allowed them to argue that the war on Iraq was about 9/11. Rapidly, the torture program was expanded to try to find a nuclear weapons program in Iraq. Colin Powell's disgraceful performance at the United Nations with a vial in his hand, using false information elicited through torture, trying to make the case to the United Nations for a war on Iraq. Powell, who had been thought to have some degree of integrity, presented a range of fabrications about Iraq's nuclear weapons program, which did not exist. After the invasion, the United States went on a massive search for nuclear weapons or other weapons of mass destruction. Nothing. Exactly as the UN investigators—such as Hans Blix, the Swedish diplomat who headed the UN team—had been saying; Blix was saying that his team had investigated everything and found nothing. A couple of months into the occupation, the United States had to concede that they had the wrong answer to Blair's "single question." Something interesting happened: the "single question" was forgotten. George W. Bush gave a speech to say that we had invaded Iraq to bring democracy to the country, to advance a "Freedom Agenda." Everyone turned around, and the press began to gush about this magnificent effort to bring democracy to the country. Practically the entire scholarly profession went along with it, with Augustus Norton being one of the few scholars to point out critically that the scholarly profession had jumped on the bandwagon but knew all along that this was nonsense.

It is true that not everyone agreed. There was some support for Bush's position in Iraq, about one percent agreed about democracy promotion. Five percent thought that the United States had invaded to help Iraqis. The rest said what was obvious to anybody with a gray cell—they had invaded to take Iraq's resources. We're not allowed to say that. We're supposed to believe that if Iraq were producing asparagus and if the center of oil production were in the South Pacific, then the United States would've invaded Iraq anyway to bring democracy. That's the official story, said with considerable uniformity across the press and academy. But the SOFA agreement finally officially brought out what had been obvious.

Iraq is now one of the most bitter, unhappy, tortured countries in the world, and the Shia–Sunni conflict, which was incubated in Iraq, is now general across the Middle

East. So, that was a great achievement of the U.S. government. The Iraqi parliament has called on the U.S. forces
to leave. But that's like being informed by world opinion. The United States will leave when the United States
decides to leave, not when the Iraqi parliament decides.
That's how it stands.

VIJAY: In 2004, UN Secretary-General Kofi Annan went
on BBC and called it an "illegal war," which you have
already referenced.[5] In January 2005, George W. Bush
said in his second inaugural address, "The survival of liberty in our land increasingly depends on the success of
liberty in other lands." There was a lot of hue and cry in
the Washington think tanks about the "Freedom Agenda"
and about "democracy promotion." All of this seemed to
run aground for the United States when Hamas won the
Palestinian elections in January 2006. U.S. Secretary of
State Condoleezza Rice told the Fatah leadership that
they must overthrow the Hamas leadership in Gaza; Rice
organized for the United Arab Emirates to do emergency
training for Fatah and for Egypt to send arms to the fighters. When Fatah revolted against Hamas in 2007, it was
a rebuke to the U.S. "democracy promotion" strategy.
Seems "liberty in other lands" was only going to work if

the political leadership in other lands was sufficiently pliant to the United States' overall agenda.

In April 2006, months after the Palestinian elections and months before the Israeli attack on Lebanon, you went to West Point and gave a very important speech on "just war" theory. The U.S. government was afflicted by a constant need to validate the war in Iraq on grounds of democracy or some form of justice. Why don't they just come out and say, *We're here for the oil*? Trump said so to Kelly Evans of the *Wall Street Journal* in 2011. "I would take the oil," he said. But that's neither here nor there. Tell me a little bit about the contradictions of the whole "just war" business, which seems to give credence to the U.S. myth around its war making.

NOAM: The talk at West Point was interesting. I was just invited to talk to a philosophy class, but there was so much interest among the student body that they opened it up to the entire cadet corps. I talked to about half the cadet corps and lots of high military officials. It was a very interesting audience, not much different from any college audience, since they were interested and asked good questions. After the talk, cadets came up and asked, *Do you think we're doing the right thing by going into the army?* and asking me, *Can you sign my book?* Usual kinds of things that I get at these kinds of talks. It was interesting to talk to them, particularly about the theory of the just war. In the 1990s, the just war business, along with humanitarian intervention, became a major topic. I don't think it is accidental. Before 1990–91, there was an easy excuse for any atrocity, any invasion, any aggression, any massacre; whatever you did, you would say, *the Russians are coming.* That was sufficient. You didn't need any fancy excuses. After the USSR collapsed, you couldn't say that the Russians were coming. After 1991, you needed something new. Well, along came "humanitarian intervention," which became a new mantra, and "just war" theory. The "just war" theory has a history. In 1977, Michael Walzer, a professor at the Institute for Advanced Study in Princeton, published a book called *Just and Unjust Wars.* I reviewed it the following year for *Inquiry.* It was basically a plea for Israeli atrocities. Most of his book, which is highly praised, largely repeats the United Nations Charter, saying yes, you can't launch an aggressive war, you must have UN Security Council authorizations and other such anodyne points. But the book gets interesting when he lays out his exceptions. Walzer goes over a couple thousand years of war and then says that there are a few cases where the argument for war was so obvious that it does not need to be discussed. The U.S. response after Pearl Harbor did not require any legitimation. Nor did the Normandy invasion. It did not need an argument. He gives about half a dozen cases of these kinds of attacks. One of them is Israel's preemptive war against Egypt and Syria in 1967. That one is so obviously right that we don't have to talk about it, he suggests. By the time Walzer wrote the book, he knew that Israel had expected to win in a couple of days and that U.S. intelligence had made it clear that there'd be little resistance from Egypt or Syria. Preemptive war is illegal, criminal, so an argument had to be made for why the Israelis conducted a preemptive war that they expected to win easily. Walzer cites an Israeli book that conducts a staged discussion amongst Israeli soldiers, where they talk about how noble they are and how they hate to shoot anybody but are forced to do so. It is so painful to them to shoot anyone, an attitude that allows Walzer to show that the Israel Defense Forces (IDF) is a uniquely moral army and the IDF wars are inherently just wars. That's basically Walzer's book from 1977.

By the 1990s, the ideas of just and unjust war and humanitarian intervention became a big deal for reasons that are not surprising. The issue was raised during the invasion of Serbia and Kosovo, when there was going to be this fantastic NATO-led humanitarian intervention that would show how marvelous the Europeans and the United States are. The facts are exactly the reverse of what was portrayed and what continues to be portrayed. In Serbia and Kosovo, there were perfectly good negotiating options. The United States invaded with the complete knowledge that the invasion was going to sharply escalate atrocities. The Clinton administration was briefed on that by Wesley Clark, the NATO general, before the war. In fact, Clark said the same thing at a press conference, where he said that the Serbians were going to react on the ground when the bombing started and there would be a massive increase in atrocities. Before the bombing, it was an unpleasant situation with a mixed story about atrocities. The invasion was undertaken with the understanding that it was going to escalate atrocities, which did escalate. The increased atrocities were used as a justification for the invasion, just reversing the timing, which is almost uniform as a practice. Even the Goldstone Commission, which investigated the war, inverted the chronology, saying that it was a humanitarian invasion because of the atrocities, which were the anticipated result of the invasion and not its cause.

VIJAY: Even the Goldstone report had to admit that the intervention was illegal because it did not have a UN Security Council resolution; it did say, however, that it was "politically and morally legitimate."

NOAM: That becomes important in what follows. Out of the war in Yugoslavia and the discussions about humanitarian intervention in the 1990s came a new doctrine called Right to Protect, or R2P. The way the R2P doctrine is treated in the international affairs literature and in the media is extremely interesting. There are actually two versions of R2P, which are shaped by this distinction between illegal wars, due to no UN Security Council resolution and yet "politically and morally legitimate" wars. One version is the official United Nations version, which was codified by a UN General Assembly resolution from 2006. If there is internal repression in a country and there is pressure for an intervention, no use of military force from outside can be used without a Security Council authorization. That's the official version of R2P. The other version comes out of a Canadian commission headed by Gareth Evans, the former, very hawkish, Australian foreign minister who had strongly supported Australia's backing of the Indonesian invasion of East Timor. The

Evans commission version of R2P, published in 2001 as the *Report of the International Commission on Intervention and State Sovereignty*, is almost exactly the same as the official version, with one key difference. There's a paragraph in it that says regional military alliances can carry out military interventions in their own region without the authorization of the UN Security Council. So, in this case, the intervention in Kosovo would not be "illegal" because NATO, a regional alliance, carried it out.

Who is the one regional military organization that can do such interventions? Well, NATO. What's their region? Not the North Atlantic, which is in the name, but the world. So, R2P means keeping to the UN Charter with one exception, which is that NATO can invade and destroy any country that it wants, as it did in Yugoslavia. NATO, of course, means the United States, with others dragged along without a UN Security Council authorization. If you look at the literature on this, any R2P intervention is justified by appeal to the UN version, but it takes place along the lines of the Evans version: an appeal to the UN Charter, but action based on the Evans–NATO exceptions. It's a pretty neat propaganda achievement. We have humanitarian intervention, which means we can attack anyone we want because we say that it is humanitarian, and it is given legitimacy because the UN had an R2P resolution supporting it, except it said you can't do it without a UN Security Council resolution, but that's a minor difficulty. This is the ideology of the willingness to accept reflexively what appear to be official doctrines that are supportive of state violence.

Kofi Annan said that the U.S. war on Iraq was a crime. That's a textbook case of a crime—a war of aggression—for which Nazi war criminals were hanged. There was no credible pretext for the invasion, no UN Security Council authorization, overwhelming opposition of the world's population, no possible redeeming feature. Hitler invaded Poland based on the "wild terror of the Poles," who had to be repressed in the name of peace. When Hitler took the Sudetenland, he said it was to bring peace and security to an area where people were in conflict, and where the Nazis would bring . . . the advantages of German civilization. That's about as credible a justification as that given by Washington for its invasion of Iraq. In the entire mainstream commentary on Iraq, you will not find one person saying that the war on Iraq was the same kind of crime as the war of aggression of Germany, which resulted in the Nuremberg trials. What you will find is someone like Obama calling the invasion of Iraq a "strategic blunder," which is what the Nazi generals said after the Battle of Stalingrad. Others who said they didn't like the war in Iraq are being greatly praised for their courage and integrity. Try to find one of them who says that the attack on Iraq was a criminal endeavor. If we take the Nuremberg trials seriously, then these people who engineered the Iraq War should be tried on the Nuremberg principle. The chief U.S. prosecutor at Nuremberg, Justice Robert Jackson, said something very interesting at the end of the proceedings: "We are handing these defendants a 'poisoned chalice,' and if we carry out similar crimes we must suffer the same consequences, or else this Tribunal is a farce." Well, you can draw your own conclusions from this statement.

VIJAY: In the West Point speech, you quoted Tacitus: "The strong do as they will. The weak suffer as they must." You often quote Tacitus, including the other line that you've used many times, "You make it a desert and call it peace." For the past decade, there's been barely any serious commentary on the situation in Iraq, whose people struggle through the detritus of the war. If we reverse the Tacitus quote, *make it a jungle, and call it war*, then it suggests how the United States seems to always find a reason to remain in Iraq. It bombs Iraq in 1991, it maintains a pretty ruthless sanctions regime during the 1990s, it bombs Iraq again in 2003, and then invades and occupies it off and on for the next several years. The reasons for this long war against Iraq are legion: the Iraqi invasion of Kuwait, the threat of Iraq's weapons of mass destruction, the need to create democracy, the threats from al-Qaeda and then ISIS, the need to protect the Kurds, and so on. These excuses come in bursts, and then some of them vanish. The example of the Kurds is exemplary because their role has also been instrumental for U.S. power. What is your sense, Noam, of the Kurdish enclave in the north of Iraq and the role that it has played since 1991?

NOAM: In 1991, after the United States drove the Iraqi army out of Kuwait, Iraqis rose up to try to overthrow the remnants of Saddam's regime. The United States bombed the Iraqi soldiers as they fled northward, massacring many during their retreat along what was later called the Highway of Death. The United States encouraged the Iraqis to rise up and to overthrow the government. People in southern Iraq, where the United States had been bombing, did launch an insurrection against Saddam, who turned his army against them and carried out a huge massacre while the United States stood by. The United States urged the revolt, and then when Saddam crushed them, the United States said that we can't do anything about it since we don't intervene in other countries. There was some negative comment about it, with some liberals asking for the United States to intervene, but nothing really happened. That was as far as it got in the south of Iraq.

The coverage changed when there was an uprising in the north, where the Iraqi Kurds live. You had Western reporters saying, *here are these blue-eyed children being attacked by this monster*, and so on. Bush had to do something, so he set up a "no-fly zone," which was actually a good thing to do, although the reasons were horrible. Under the no-fly zone, the northern Iraqi Kurds attained a significant element of independence. Unfortunately, what's going on internally amongst the Kurds is not pretty, since there are two groups that are corrupt and brutal. They did not make use of the opportunity to advance anything, but at least they were free from Saddam's attacks in 1991.

These attacks against the Kurds were horrendous, major crimes. The worst by far were committed in the 1980s, during the Anfal campaign, including the gassing of Kurds in the town of Halabja in 1988 (which came alongside the chemical warfare against Iran). The invasion of Kuwait, though a serious crime, added little to the Iraqi government's already horrendous record. Saddam, however, in the 1980s remained a favored ally and trading partner of the United States, Britain, and West Germany, which further abetted these crimes. The Reagan administration even sought to prevent congressional reaction to the gassing of the Kurds, including the failed plea of Senate Foreign Relations Committee chair Claiborne Pell that "we cannot be silent on genocide again." So extreme was Reagan's support for Saddam that when the ABC correspondent Charles Glass revealed the site of one of Saddam's biological warfare programs a few months after Halabja, Washington denied the facts, and the story died.

These attacks on the Kurds were now prevented by the no-fly zone. The Kurds have been brutally and viciously repressed throughout the region. Most of the Kurds are in Turkey, where the repression has been the worst. The no-fly zone over northern Iraq came at the same time as the United States increased military aid to Turkey, which then conducted a monstrous assault on Kurds in the southeast of that country. This was under President Clinton. By 1998, when the terror against the Kurds peaked, U.S. aid was at its highest. There was no coverage of any of this, with the *New York Times* largely silent (this is even though it had a bureau and a very good reporter—Stephen Kinzer—in the country. Kinzer would later write very well about these issues). Basically, what was happening in the southeast of Turkey to the Kurds was suppressed. You can find a few things here and there, but not much.

I visited Turkey in February 2002, at the tail end of this cycle of atrocities. I visited with a couple of very courageous Kurdish human rights activists, many sent to prison and tortured but still at it. I won't mention the names of these amazing people, but I went with them to Diyarbakir, the main Kurdish city. We were followed by Turkish security forces, who were pretty overt about their surveillance. If my Turkish friends saw kids playing in the streets with clothes that suggested the Kurdish flag, they led me in a different direction, because if we went there, they said, then the families would be subjected to violent repression. People were afraid to talk. I gave a speech there on some of the themes that emerge from the war on terror, as it were. People asked many questions, including about whether the United States would go to war against Iraq and what this would mean for the Kurds.

VIJAY: That interaction in Diyarbakir was recorded. The answer you gave to the person who asks about the possibility of a full-scale U.S. attack on Iraq is worth recounting:

NOAM: This is an important issue that is on the agenda nowadays. There are two kinds of reasons for a possible U.S. attack on Iraq. The first is domestic, internal to the United States. If you were an advisor to the Bush administration, what would you say? Would you say, "Try to focus people's attention on the Enron scandal, and the fact that the proposed tax cuts for the rich will undermine all social programs and will leave most of the population in serious trouble"? Is that what you want the people to pay attention to, policies like these? Obviously not. What you want is for people to be frightened, to huddle under the umbrella of power, not to pay attention to what you are doing to them while serving the interests of narrow rich-and-powerful sectors. So, you want to have a military conflict. That's the domestic side. On the international side, Iraq has the second largest reserves of oil in the world. The first is Saudi Arabia, Iraq is the second. The United States certainly will not give up control of this huge source of power and wealth. Furthermore, right now, if the Iraqi oil were to come back into the international system, it would be largely under the control of Russia, France, and others,

134

not U.S. energy companies. And the United States is not going to permit that. So, we can be pretty confident that one way or another the United States is trying to ensure that Iraq will reenter the international system under U.S. control. Now, how do you achieve this? Well, one plan, and this plan has been discussed in Turkey, as you know, is for the United States to use Turkey as a mercenary military force to conquer northern Iraq with ground troops while the United States bombs from twenty thousand feet. The compensation for Turkey could be that it will get control of the oil resources of Mosul and Kirkuk, which it has always regarded as part of Turkey. And for the United States, that will block its enemies—Russia, France, and others—from having privileged access to the oil of that region. Meanwhile, the United States will take over the south in some fashion. What happens to the Kurds? I hate to think about it. It will probably be a terrible slaughter of one kind or another. They will be right in the middle of this. For Turkey, apart from the question of right and wrong, it would be a very dangerous move. And it's a very dangerous move for the United States as well, if only because it could blow up the whole region. It could lead to a revolution in Saudi Arabia. Nobody knows. Elements of the Bush administration are pursuing these and similar plans, and you can see the logic. Whether they will be allowed to implement such plans is another story. I'm rather skeptical. I think the arguments against it are probably too strong. But they don't know themselves, and surely no one else can.

A human rights activist in Istanbul took me to the slums, which were horrendous. In Istanbul, most people don't know that these exist, since they are where the middle class does not go, and they are full of refugees, hundreds of thousands, perhaps millions. They fled from the Kurdish areas in Turkey's southeast and ended up in these living conditions. A family lives in a tiny room, the father afraid to go out because he might be killed, the children forced to go to work; I hated to ask them where the children are working, but at least they survive and bring in a little bit of money. This is some of the most horrible misery I've ever seen, and I've seen a lot in my travels. Hundreds of thousands of Kurds driven out of their homes due to U.S. weapons sent by the Clinton administration. Absolute silence about these matters. I visited Turkey a few more times, and things seemed a little better in terms of the bitter attacks on the Kurdish areas, not as bad as the 1990s, I mean. A horrible record of repression.

VIJAY: The war that the Kurdish people in Diyarbakir asked you about in February 2002 did take place a year later. It destabilized the entire region, opening what appeared to be avenues for regional powers to complete projects that had been stalled. Many of these attempts failed drastically. The Turkish government, for instance, hoped to finally crush the Kurdish Question and to seize parts of Syria that it had long considered part of Turkish territory. This was partly the motivation for the Turkish government during the war against Syria that began in 2011. But it failed, since the Kurdish Question did not close, nor did Turkey get to keep those parts of Syria that it had seized for a time. The one lasting transformation due to the U.S. war on Iraq in 2003 seems not to regard Turkish power, but to regard the role of Iran in the region. Iran developed considerable influence in Iraq and Syria and deepened its links with Lebanon. During this period, the United States tried to push Iran back to its borders. There was the Syria Accountability Act of 2005, which the United States used as an instrument to punish Syria for its links to Iran; there's the U.S.-authorized Israeli attack on Lebanon in 2006, with emphasis on Hezbollah; then out of nowhere came the "nuclear issues," with Iran coming under intense sanctions by the United States and the Europeans. Could you reflect a little bit on this attempt to push Iran back to its borders?

NOAM: To push Iran back to its borders means to push its influence back. Iran didn't invade Lebanon. Lebanon is a plural society, with a large Shia population that has close ties with Iran (not just theological but also family ties). Hezbollah is basically the main force of the Shia community in Lebanon. Iran didn't invade Iraq. It's the other way around, since Iraq invaded Iran in 1980. But there has been a long-standing influence of Iran, through its Shia religious connections, on Iraq. The Iranian threat, as the United States sees it, is like the China threat: they're spreading their influence. Like China, Iran does not follow U.S. orders. It used to do so under the shah, and then all was well. In fact, speaking of nuclear weapons, the shah of Iran said that he would develop nuclear weapons, and the United States supported him. A decade later, the United States invited Iraqi nuclear engineers for advanced training as part of an attempt to deliver nuclear weapons to Iraq. If you are a pliable ruling elite, then all is well; if you don't follow orders, be careful. Iran did not have a nuclear weapons program until after the Iraqi invasion in 1980 and the subsequent chemical attacks. Ayatollah

Khomeini, who released a *fatwa* against such weapons, nonetheless obviously felt that Iran had to have a way to defend itself. This program ran till 2003, when Khatami ended it. Since then, Iran has developed nuclear power, with no evidence that they are trying to develop nuclear weapons or to develop nuclear weapons capability. That's something that many countries have, but Iran does not have it.

Let's look carefully at the nuclear weapons issue, which developed in the 2000s. Is there a threat of Iranian nuclear weapons? Suppose Iran did have nuclear weapons—what would the threat be? If Iran tried to mount a nuclear weapon onto a missile, the country would be vaporized. They could not do a thing with a nuclear weapon except use it as deterrence. That's a problem for the United States. You can't allow a country you're trying to destroy have a deterrent capacity. Nevertheless, let's pretend for the sake of discussion that there is a nuclear weapons threat from Iran. Is there a way to end it? The simple way would be to establish a nuclear weapons free zone in the Middle East. There are such zones around the world. They can't function, because the United States violates every one of them by putting nuclear weapons on foreign military bases or by harboring submarines that have these

139

weapons. There's an African Nuclear Weapons Free Zone Treaty based on the Pelindaba Treaty (2009), which the United States violates by turning, with British support, the colonial island of Diego Garcia into a military base with nuclear facilities. So, it can't be established. There's one in the Pacific, and this can't go into effect because the United States insists on nuclear weapons facilities on specific islands. The most important would be the Middle East Nuclear Weapons Free Zone. Why not institute it with intensive inspections by the International Atomic Energy Agency (IAEA), which we know would work? We already have experience under the JCPOA (Joint Comprehensive Plan of Action), the Iran nuclear deal, which worked until the United States pulled out of it unilaterally. There are intensive inspections, including by U.S. intelligence, worked into the plan. Let's have a nuclear weapons free zone with intensive inspections. Is there a problem instituting it? Not really. The Arab states have been demanding it for twenty-five years. Iran strongly supports it. The G77, about 130 countries of the global south, very strongly support it. Europe raised no objections. So, what's the problem? Well, the usual one. The United States won't allow it. The United States vetoes any suggestion of it in international forums. Obama vetoed it in 2015 when it came up during the conference of the nonproliferation treaty. Since then, the United States has blocked it.

Why does the United States block this treaty? Everybody knows why, and nobody says anything aloud, except in arms-control circles. If the treaty is accepted, then Israel's nuclear weapons facilities would have to be inspected. The *New York Times* came out with its first editorial in which it said, Hey we have this bright idea: *why not establish a nuclear weapons free zone in the Middle East and end the Iranian threat?*[6] Then comes the footnote: Israel's nuclear weapons are nonnegotiable. We can have a nuclear weapons free zone, except the one state that has a big arsenal of nuclear weapons will not be in it. The United States does not even formally concede that Israel has nuclear weapons. But at least the *Times* mentioned it; first time I've seen it mentioned in these kinds of publications. The United States does not concede it due to the implications of U.S. law. If a state develops nuclear weapons outside the framework of international agreements, then there are legal issues—such as the Symington Amendment—that might ban U.S. transfers of a range of economic and military assistance to that state. Acknowledgment of Israel's nuclear weapons program, developed outside the IAEA, would mean that the United States would have to stop its subsidies to Israel and stop its military cooperation. Nobody wants to open that door. If there was a serious Palestinian solidarity movement in the United States, it would be pressing for this acknowledgment. So, there is a simple way to handle the potential Iranian nuclear weapons program, but nobody pushes it because this is not the objective.

VIJAY: In 2015, when Iran signed the JCPOA, Iran's foreign minister, Jawad Zarif, said, "The whole of the Middle East must rid itself of nuclear weapons." That would have been the perfect opportunity to advance the idea of the Middle East Nuclear Weapons Free Zone, which had been put on the table by Egypt and Iran in 1974. There are currently five nuclear weapons free zones:

1. Treaty for the Prohibition of Nuclear Weapons in Latin America and the Caribbean (Treaty of Tlatelolco), 1967
2. Treaty on the Southeast Asia Nuclear Weapons Free Zone (Treaty of Bangkok), 1977
3. South Pacific Nuclear-Free Zone Treaty (Treaty of Rarotonga), 1986

4. African Nuclear Weapons Free Zone Treaty (Treaty of Pelindaba), 2009

5. Treaty on a Nuclear Weapon Free Zone in Central Asia, 2009

Iran is a member of the Nuclear Non-Proliferation Treaty (NPT). Its status as a nuclear power state is guaranteed by the NPT. It is on that basis that the International Atomic Energy Agency (IAEA) monitors Iran's nuclear industry. But meanwhile, Israel is not a member of the NPT, has no IAEA monitors, and yet has a growing nuclear arsenal. It is important to indicate that despite its policy of "studied ambiguity" (*amimut*), Israel is a known nuclear weapons state, not a nuclear energy state. The United States has known of Israel's nuclear weapons program since July 1960. By December of that year, a U.S. government Special National Intelligence Estimate (SNIE 100-8-60) acknowledged that Israel "is engaged in construction of a nuclear reactor complex in the Negev near Beersheba" and that "plutonium production for weapons is at least one major purpose of this effort." By 1969, the Nixon administration had sufficient evidence that Israel had reached the point "whereby all the components for a weapon are at hand, awaiting only final assembly and testing." In a memorandum from July 19, 1969, Nixon's

143

secretary of state, Henry Kissinger, wrote, "We judge that the introduction of nuclear weapons into the Near East would increase the dangers in an already dangerous situation and therefore not in our interest." But Kissinger was wary of making Israel's nuclear weapons program an issue. "Our main object is to keep secret Israeli nuclear weapons," he concluded his memorandum to Nixon. This has remained U.S. policy since then. It was Norway that provided Israel with the heavy water in 1959, and it would be its neighbor Finland that tried to rein in Israeli nuclear weapons in 2012. A proposed Middle East Nuclear Weapons Free Zone conference to be held in Helsinki in December 2012 was scuttled by Israeli pressure. The 189 member nations of the NPT—including Iran—said they would attend. Israel refused. There are three other states, apart from Israel, that are not in the NPT: India, Pakistan, and South Sudan. In September 2013, Iran's president Hassan Rouhani told the UN General Assembly that Israel should join the NPT "without further delay." This was met in Tel Aviv with stone silence. As you say, Noam, the scofflaw of the region—Israel—refuses to accept international agreements or to help create a zone of peace in West Asia. But it is not alone. The United States currently houses nuclear weapons in its bases along the Gulf, from

Bahrain to Qatar and outward to Djibouti. A Middle East Nuclear Weapons Free Zone would mean an end to the U.S. practice of housing tactical nuclear weapons in the waters around the region. In May 2015, the United States and the United Kingdom killed off the final document of a conference of the NPT states because of the concept of the Middle East Nuclear Weapons Free Zone. Each Arab state and Iran agreed to the concept, despite the otherwise fractious divides in the region. Only Israel and the West raised objections to it. It tells one a great deal about who maintains and monitors the roadblocks to peace in West Asia.

NOAM: Israel does not want anything like a nuclear weapons free zone. It does not want a deterrent in West Asia. Israel regularly bombs Syria, it invaded Lebanon numerous times, it continues the occupation of the Palestinians. I've seen the extremely harmful effects of Israeli policy several times. Israel simply does not want a deterrent in the region.

Iran is a small-scale version of China. It does not get intimidated and does not follow orders. Iran might be able to develop some kind of deterrent, but the United States and Israel do not want that. The nuclear weapons problem can be easily handled if Israel stops being a sacred cow that can't be touched.

VIJAY: If the Middle East Nuclear Weapons Free Zone is one way to build the process for peace in the region, another would be a grand bargain between Saudi Arabia and Iran. It is incorrect to assume that the antipathy between Saudi Arabia and Iran is sectarian. After all, when the shah of Iran was in charge in Tehran, that monarch and the Saudi monarchs had no problem having a close equation. Matters fell apart when the Iranian people got rid of their monarch and created an Islamic Republic, which challenged the Saudi monarchy frontally. Again, such a bargain between Iran and Saudi Arabia, which goes on and off the table, is opposed by the United States and Israel.

NOAM: The U.S. position has been very clear. It was actually formalized by Trump in his one geopolitical achievement, the Abraham Accords. Technically, these accords did not draw in Saudi Arabia, but effectively they did. This is a formal agreement among the most reactionary states in the region: Israel, the United Arab Emirates (UAE), Bahrain, and Morocco. The UAE, Bahrain, and Morocco normalized relations with Israel. Sudan was forced into it because the United States told them that if they did not, then they would return to the terrorist list. Arms deals were cut with the UAE and Morocco to seal the deal. Part of the deal was Trump's authorization of Morocco's illegal takeover of Western Sahara in violation of international law. Morocco has a virtual monopoly on phosphates, an irreplaceable mineral that is vital for agriculture; Western Sahara has phosphates, which now extends Morocco's monopoly. This Abraham alliance combined resource control with military muscle and technical capacity (the latter mainly from Israel). Egypt was not formally part of it, but Egypt has an open relationship with Israel. This is an alliance of reactionary states, which is a core part of Steve Bannon's international program, but it is inherent in the U.S. policy of trying to create alliances of the most reactionary states, which are the basis for U.S. power.

Part of this arc of reactionary states are those of the Abraham Accords, plus Egypt, plus Saudi Arabia, plus Orban's Hungary, plus Bolsonaro's Brazil, plus Modi's India (perfect member, destroying secular democracy, creating a Hindu ethnocracy, crushing Kashmir). That's the alliance. In the Middle East, it is directed against Iran.

In Latin America, it is directed against Cuba and Venezuela. Meanwhile, in all these parts of the world, regional powers are trying to dial back the tension. Saudi Arabia and Iran are moving toward cutting back the hostility and establishing relations. In Latin America, the new mood in the Community of Latin American and Caribbean States (CELAC) is illustrative. This is going to undercut U.S. policy in these regions, which is why the United States is going to work hard to prevent it.

VIJAY: Ten years ago, I was in Doha speaking to a senior intelligence official of the Qatari government. We were on the corniche that looks out toward Iran, which you can actually see at times. He said to me, *We have a real problem of drinking water in Qatar.* Half of Qatar's water comes from desalination, while the rest comes from aquifers (shared with Saudi Arabia). *Fifteen years ago*, he said, which means in the 1990s, *we had planned to build a pipeline from Iran to Qatar to carry fresh water.* This sounded like a fantasy to me, but then what do I know? He said, *You-know-who blocked it.* I said, *Why did you go along with you-know-who?* Qatar has an enormous U.S. military presence, making the emirate effectively beholden to the United States. A few days later, he drove me down the road toward Saudi Arabia, and as we neared the base our car was stopped, and we were told to go back to Doha. *You used to be a senior Qatari intelligence official*, I said to him. *Yes*, he said, smiling, *but the key word here is* Qatari.

NOAM: That's how you show your muscle.

4

Libya

VIJAY: Walking amidst the ruins of the Arab Spring in Tahrir Square in Cairo, Egypt, about two years after the mass demonstrations in 2011, it was clear to me that a combination of local oligarchs, military top brass, and the Western countries simply did not want to see the development of democratic regimes in countries such as Egypt. It was unacceptable. A true democracy in Egypt, for instance, would annul the peace deal with Israel, since that is the general mood in the country. An Egyptian democracy would not be willing to take orders from the United States or Saudi Arabia when it came to its relations on the African continent. Even the risk of these things happening was far too much to allow. The United States tried to get President Hosni Mubarak to negotiate with the crowds. Obama's envoy Frank Wisner Jr. arrived in Cairo as Tahrir overflowed to tell Mubarak to make modest concessions to prevent the advancement of democracy. The crowd would not have it. Mubarak went. But the United States—behind the scenes—ensured that the military remained in control, pulling the strings, preventing the start of a new constitution-writing process that would have democratized society. The fig leaf fell off two years later, when General Abd al-Fatah el-Sisi became President Abd al-Fatah el-Sisi, leaving his military fatigues but

153

keeping in place military power. The next year, Egypt's interior minister, General Mohammed Ibrahim, made a casual statement which offered a sense of the smugness of Egypt's ruling elite: "We are living a golden age of unity between the judges, the police, and the army."

Further west, in Libya, the country had been torn apart by the NATO bombing of 2011, which left the way clear for the return of the most reactionary Islamist groups and for the entry of an old CIA-backed general who became the willing pawn of Saudi Arabia, Egypt, France, and Russia. My old friends in Benghazi began to caution me to not return to the country, and in the midst of those cautions some of them lost their lives. Early into the uprisings in Tunisia and Egypt, you gave a series of interviews in which you spoke about the importance of the mass demonstrations, but you doubted that the United States would permit them to advance to create democratic state structures. NATO's war in Libya, which began in March 2011, a month after Egypt's Mubarak resigned, muddied the entire dynamic (the armed struggle in Syria began a few days before the NATO bombing commenced). The NATO assault on Libya has not been properly understood, indeed NATO's global role is poorly understood. The NATO war was a horrendous war, which shifted the dial of the so-called Arab Spring from peaceful demonstration to civil war to imperialist attack. In 2014, you said, "NATO's official mission is to control the world." Seems like NATO's participation in the war on Afghanistan (2001) and in the war on Libya (2011) illustrates this mission to control the world.

NOAM: Until the collapse of the USSR in 1991, there was at least a moderately plausible rationale for NATO. It claimed to be a defensive alliance, defending Western Europe against what was said to be Soviet aggression. We can discuss how credible that pretext was, but at least it had an element of rationality behind it. After the USSR collapsed, the pretext collapsed with it. So, what's NATO in the aftermath of the USSR? Just before the USSR collapsed, there were discussions between George H. W. Bush and James Baker in the United States, Helmut Kohl and Hans-Dietrich Genscher in Germany, and Mikhail Gorbachev in the USSR, trying to work out what the world should look like in a post-USSR world. Gorbachev's vision was for a unified Eurasia, an integrated zone of peace from the Atlantic to the Pacific. The immediate issue was what to do with Germany. For Russia, Germany is not a small problem, since Germany virtually destroyed

Russia repeatedly during the preceding century. If Germany is part of a hostile military alliance against Russia, then it puts that country in extreme danger. Bush and Baker, with the limited support of the Germans, called for unifying Germany, and Gorbachev agreed to it with one important concession: that NATO move not one inch to the east of the German border. Nobody was talking about anything beyond that. It was a tacit understanding, which can be read in the German archives. Bush and Baker wanted U.S. forces to move into the former East Germany, which they did, while Kohl and Genscher were not keen on such an expansion. Gorbachev objected. But the United States pointed out that this was a gentleman's agreement, and it was never on paper; there is no document that says NATO will not move to the east. *If you're dumb enough to accept our word of honor,* they implied, *that's your problem.* The best study of these discussions was published in *International Security*, authored by Joshua Itzkowitz Shifrinson, who argued that Bush and Baker consciously deceived Gorbachev.[1]

So, NATO forces moved to East Germany. Clinton came along and expanded NATO further eastward, toward the Russian border. Ukraine entered NATO's Partnership for Peace program in 1994 and then was offered membership by the United States in 2008 (this offer was blocked by France and Germany). When Russia was weakened by the fall of the USSR, Russians accepted things imposed on them by the United States. As Russia regained its strength, particularly under Vladimir Putin, these impositions by the United States were not accepted anymore, and a red line was drawn.

NATO was restructured. They had to have a new mission. Anders Fogh Rasmussen, the former prime minister of Denmark, was then secretary-general of NATO. In 2014, he said that NATO's new role was to protect the global energy system. Well, "energy security" means control the whole world, since there are pipelines everywhere and since there is maritime passage everywhere. NATO weaponized the idea of "human rights" to give it the unique right to intervene anywhere, using the Gareth Evans version of R2P, namely that NATO—as a regional organization—had the right to intervene without a UN Security Council resolution. NATO means the United States. Nobody does anything in NATO unless the United States initiates it; then, other powers can decide whether to go along with it. The idea was to reconstruct NATO to make the United States the global hegemon, which it already was in terms of power, but this formalized it. So, it is not merely NATO's official mission to control the world, but NATO was reconstructed as the instrument for the United States to try to control the world.

VIJAY: Three of the major interventions outside western Europe that the United States initiated after the collapse of the USSR—namely, in Yugoslavia (1999), Afghanistan (2001), and Libya (2011)—were not done directly as U.S. intervention but came under the guise of a NATO intervention. They couldn't use NATO in Iraq because France and Germany were not prepared to go along with it. Could you lead us into this use of NATO as an instrument of U.S. power in these instances, perhaps starting with Yugoslavia and then going into Libya?

NOAM: By 1995, the situation on the ground in Yugoslavia had settled down. There were atrocities on all sides. In Bosnia, the Serbs had carried out the Srebrenica attack, about which there is a lot of information. The Croatians had carried out their attacks with U.S. support, which drove a couple of hundred thousand Serbs out of the contested territory. The situation, ugly as it was with all the mutual atrocities, had reached a kind of settlement. At that point, Clinton was able to intervene and bring the forces together to establish the Dayton Agreement under U.S. auspices. The Dayton Agreement established the United States as the dominant force in Yugoslavia. In part, this was a conflict between the United States and Europe—namely, Germany. Who was going to dominate Yugoslavia? Would it be Germany or the United States? Clinton stayed out of the conflict from 1991 (when Slovenia and Croatia seceded from Yugoslavia) until the lead-up to the Dayton conversations (the main items of the agreement had been on the table since 1992, with most parties having agreed to them). The Europeans had forces on the ground, trying to maintain the peace. The United States did not have forces on the ground. *We are going to bomb from the air*, the United States said, *but we're not going to put any forces on the ground*. The Europeans did not like that, because it meant that their forces would be targets in retaliation for the U.S. bombing. The United States used NATO as cover, with no serious internal objection. This was the same with Afghanistan, which was a U.S. war with NATO as cover.

The NATO war in Libya was different. It was initiated by France. There was a civil conflict going on in Libya, with Qaddafi's forces issuing threats against Benghazi, which was the center of the rebel uprising. At that time,

the three major powers—Britain, France, and the United
States—pushed through a United Nations Security Council resolution, which Russia did not veto—didn't support
it, but didn't veto it either. Nor did China. The resolution
was limited. It said that the UN authorized the establishment of a no-fly zone to curtail the conflict and that the
two sides should move toward a negotiation. Qaddafi formally accepted that. The African Union had its own pro-
posal to move forward toward negotiations, but they were
simply dismissed. Nobody paid attention to that, so what
does Africa have to say about what happens in Africa?
They were set aside.

VIJAY: That dismissal of the African Union is important to
this story. The African Union (AU) engaged with the Libyan conflict from its start in February 2011. But the AU was
both outflanked by the Western powers and hampered by
the incoherence of its own member states. For instance,
on March 17, 2011, three African states (Gabon, Nigeria, and South Africa) voted for the second UN Security
Council resolution 1973, which allowed "member states"
to use "all necessary measures" under Chapter VII of the
UN Charter; this resolution effectively opened the door
for the United States, France, or both under NATO col-

ors to bomb Libya. Each of these states could have voted against the resolution or at least abstained from the vote, but instead they voted for it (Brazil, Germany, India, China, and Russia abstained; no country voted against it). The African states gave cover for an imperialist attack on a fellow African state. France led the bombing of Libya two days later, on March 19.

On the same day as the bombing began, the African Union's High-Level Ad hoc Committee on Libya—which included President Jacob Zuma of South Africa, who had voted for the resolution two days before—released a communiqué calling for all sides to stop the fighting and for political reforms in Libya. The tone of the communiqué is dated, since the bombing had already begun by the time it was released. In the communiqué, the African Union indicated something significant that has received minimal commentary:

The members of the High-Level ad hoc Committee expressed their regret of not being able, as they had envisaged, to travel to Libya, on 20 March 2011, to meet the parties, both of which had agreed to deal with it. The Committee, in conformity with resolution 1973 (2011) of the United Nations Security Council, requested the required permission for the

161

*flight carrying its members to Libya, in order to fulfill their
mandate. The Committee was denied permission.*

The communiqué's key sentence is written in passive
voice. Who "denied permission"? This has never been
officially clarified. Officials at that time told me, however,
that they were informed by NATO command that the
bombing was going to proceed, and that the safety of their
flight into Libya could not be guaranteed. In other words,
the West prevented the African Union from attempting
to use "all measures" to bring the parties to the table
before the war escalated by NATO bombing. The African
Union delegation did not arrive in Tripoli, Libya, until
April 11, when Jacob Zuma led a five-member team to
speak with Qaddafi. As the bombs continued to pummel
Libya, Qaddafi agreed to the African Union road map to
peace. Zuma, who met with Qaddafi, told the press that
Qaddafi would proceed to a cease-fire as soon as the deal
had been agreed to in Benghazi by the rebel leadership.
However, given the advantage of the NATO air cover, the
rebel leadership refused when the African Union delegation came to Benghazi.

It is telling that the French philosopher Bernard-Henri
Lévy, who flew to Benghazi in March, was able to bring

sections of the Benghazi rebel leadership to meet French president Nicholas Sarkozy on March 10, but the African Union leadership was not permitted a proper discussion with them. This Benghazi leadership, by the way, was made up of financial advisors to the Gulf Arab emirs and Libyan businessmen who had lived in the West for decades. Sarkozy told the Benghazi leadership that even if France did not get the proper UN Security Council resolution—which they did a week later—France would join Britain and use the cover of regional organizations (the Gareth Evans formula), such as the European Union, the Arab League, and the African Union, to attack Libya. "My resolution is total," Sarkozy told them. The decision to bomb Libya had been made long before the negotiation channels had been exhausted.

Amnesty International—led by Donatella Rovera—conducted important ground-level studies of the impact of the bombing, finding that the NATO bombing had killed uncounted numbers of civilians, obliterated the country's infrastructure, and damaged the state institutions beyond repair (one key report from March 2012 is called *The Forgotten Victims of NATO Strikes*). NATO bombed areas where Qaddafi enjoyed considerable support, which meant that NATO was bombing not merely to protect civilians but also to attack civilians who supported Qaddafi. That was a direct violation of UN Security Council resolution 1973.

NOAM: France violated Security Council resolution 1973 and became the air force of the opposition. Britain followed. What were France's motives? There was the usual posturing, with Bernard-Henri Lévy making passionate, but empty, speeches about how we have to protect human rights and about the glory of France. We can dismiss that. We don't have access to the French archives, but presumably their motives were to strengthen their own position in North and West Africa, including over Niger, from which France extracts uranium for its nuclear power plants. France also has a fantasy about its colonial legacy, so the war was like other colonial wars—brutal and harsh. Britain went along with it all, and then Obama joined, leading from behind, as he put it. Britain and the United States joined by violating the UN Security Council resolution, because they too became the air force of the opposition, bombing government targets that were far from the front lines. No negotiations were permitted, neither from the African Union nor from the United Nations. The NATO-backed opposition forces managed to conquer more territory, finally reaching Sirte, where Qaddafi was hiding, and then murdering him brutally. Hillary Clinton made her famous comment about the great triumph of murdering Qaddafi at that time, a tasteless comment worthy of imperial overlords.

Libya broke up into territories controlled by warring militia groups, a huge number of casualties, the country shattered, the people devastated. If NATO had not bombed, would there have been serious casualties in Benghazi? We don't know, but what we know is that the devastation of the war was far worse than anything that was plausibly anticipated, which might have been prevented by the African Union. The entire region—North Africa—felt the negative impact of the war. A huge flow of arms swept from Libya across North and West Africa, supporting all kinds of Islamic terrorist groups, such as ISIS and other offshoots. These wars, which hit Mali and Nigeria, then produced its own flow of migrants toward Libya and Europe, joining migrants who had already been on the road fleeing from the utter disaster that European colonialism has left in Africa. There's a good story by Ian Urbina in the *New Yorker* about the hideous concentration camps set up on the Libyan coastline, supported by the European Union, managed by criminal Libyan gangs, where they congregate refugees trying to flee to Europe.[2] They are held in there to make sure that they never get to the Mediterranean Sea. The Europeans and the United States have military bases in the Sahel to interdict migrants even before they get to Libya. If the migrants reach the Mediterranean, there are legal problems for Europe, at least formally, since the prohibition against *refoulment* [returning refugees to places where they will be persecuted] will prevent the refusal of the migrants. *Refoulment* is a serious crime under international law, so the refugees who make it to European waters have to be accepted. They want to prevent that and at the same time keep the image of Europe as a decent, law-abiding place. To do so, the Europeans fund the so-called Libyan Coast Guard, which is basically a gangster operation; this operation is given boats, equipment, and money by the Europeans. So, the Europeans send the refugees either to vicious concentration camps or back to their homelands from which they have fled because they find them unlivable (the result of hundreds of years of mostly European devastation of Africa, which is quite serious). That's Libya today.

There are two contestants for the government: the Turkish-backed government in Tripoli, which is the UN-

recognized government, and the Haftar-based government, supported by Russia (and Saudi Arabia). Despite
the illusion of these two governments, the country is an
absolute disaster area, full of war and gangs. The NATO
intervention had a devastating effect on Libya, which has
spread across the region and into the Middle East.

VIJAY: Right after the NATO bombing began to slow
down a few months after it began, many people—such
as in the UN secretariat, in human rights organizations,
and journalists—wrote to NATO to ask them to release
details of their bombing runs so as to have a clear account
of civilian casualties. It was obligatory for the UN to provide a report about UN Security Council resolution 1973.
The UN impaneled the International Commission of
Inquiry on Libya and placed the Canadian jurist Philippe
Kirsch as its chair; Kirsch had been the first president of
the International Criminal Court from 2003 to 2009, so
he knew a few things about international law and war
crimes. The commission asked NATO to provide details
on the bombing of Libya. On February 15, 2012, Peter
Olson, NATO's lead attorney, wrote to the commission to
say that NATO had not violated the letter of the UN resolution. Qaddafi, Olson wrote, had "committed serious

violations of international law," but NATO had not:

We would be concerned, however, if "NATO incidents" were included in the Commission's report as on a par with those which the Commission may ultimately conclude did violate law or constitute crimes. We note in this regard that the Commission's mandate is to discuss "the facts and circumstance of . . . violations [of law] and . . . crimes perpetrated." We would accordingly request that, in the event the Commission elects to include a discussion of NATO actions in Libya, its report clearly state that NATO did not deliberately target civilians and did not commit war crimes in Libya.

No investigation necessary, since NATO ipso facto "did not deliberately target civilians" and therefore "did not commit war crimes." Case closed.

NOAM: Olson is right. That's an axiom. NATO means the United States, and the United States cannot commit war crimes by definition. Even in the canons of international law, the United States cannot commit war crimes. When the United States agreed to jurisdiction by the World Court, it inserted a proviso that the United States was not bound by the UN Charter or the Charter of the Organization of American States [OAS]. This is the text that the United States inserted as part of the "acceptance of jurisdiction" in 1946. Those are the foundations of modern international law. The United States insisted right away that it was not to be bound by either the UN Charter or the OAS Charter, so therefore it is legally entitled to commit war crimes, even to commit genocide. When the United States signed on to the genocide convention in 1988—after a thirty-seven-year battle in the U.S. Senate—it added a proviso saying that it did not apply to the United States. The tribunal at the International Court of Justice that assessed the Yugoslav charge against NATO in 1999 permitted the United States to separate itself and not be subject to the charge, because the Yugoslav charge included the word *genocide* and the United States—by law—is entitled to carry out genocide. Across the board, the United States is legally permitted to commit any crime, and the international legal system accepts this as they must, because the World Court does accept the condition that if a country does not subject itself to court rulings, then they cannot be prosecuted. That's the way the system is set up. So, Olson was correct. NATO, meaning the United States, cannot commit war crimes.

VIJAY: It is likely that apart from experts on international law in law schools, most people know nothing about the proviso that allows the United States to extricate itself from the rules of the world. None of this is taught in schools or colleges or raised even for discussion by the media. Literacy levels about these issues are maintained at a low level almost deliberately. Nowadays in the United States there are challenges to various schools of thought—critical race theory and ethnic studies being two examples; these are seen as anti-American and therefore in need of formal suppression.

NOAM: The general public knows absolutely nothing about this. It's just not part of the educational system. If anyone dared to bring it into the educational system, they'd be denounced across the board as an anti-American communist. In the 1960s, as a result of the activism of a range of groups, the country began to become more civilized, began to be concerned about the rights of African Americans, women, workers, and began to open the door to discussions about free speech. These issues were pushed to the front of the agenda and had a big civilizing effect on U.S. society. Liberal intellectuals saw this as "the time of troubles" (the common phrase in these circles) rather than as a period of civilization. In 1973, David Rockefeller formed the Trilateral Commission, made up of members from North America, Western Europe, and Japan; they were people who represented international elite, liberal, intellectual opinion (the Carter administration was drawn from their ranks). Their first publication is called *The Crisis of Democracy* (1975). This is elite liberal opinion that condemned what happened in the 1960s because these new movements brought about a crisis of democracy. These "special interests"—youth, elderly, women, workers, farmers, minorities—who were supposed to be passive and obedient had begun to enter the public arena with their concerns and their demands. The state, they said, cannot deal with these pressures, so these special interests must revert to their obedience and passivity so that we can have a real democracy. Samuel Huntington, one of the authors of the study and a professor of political science at Harvard, said that back in the days of Harry Truman the United States was a true democracy because Wall Street and the corporate sector could run the country without interference. Huntington was a leading liberal intellectual who wanted a democracy without the noise of the special interests who had disrupted that consensus in the 1960s. There was nothing unusual in Huntington's

171

theory, since it was standard liberal, democratic theory. The Trilateral Commission was concerned that universities and churches had failed in their responsibility to "indoctrinate the young." They had failed to indoctrinate the youth into passivity and obedience, and therefore the Trilateral Commission had to change that. In fact, universities changed considerably after that to exercise more effective control and indoctrination, imposing their business models on the curriculum and on faculty members. That's the liberal end of the spectrum, which forms the cultural background to the neoliberal assault that picked up in the decades to come. Got to destroy the reservoirs of popular resistance—unions and political organizations. No interference was permitted in the rights of the very rich and the corporate sector to do what they wanted.

When the book *The Crisis of Democracy* appeared, I immediately asked the MIT library to buy a dozen copies of it because I figured it would probably go out of print as soon as anybody actually read it. That's what happened. The book very quickly went out of print. Years later, when people had forgotten about the implications of the book, it reappeared in print, so you can get a copy now. But at least MIT students could get it through subversives like me. These are critical parts of what happened in the way of major cultural changes. Effective indoctrination had to be conducted so that nobody would be taught the things we are discussing here, things that are in the public record if you learned how to find them. You'd have to search hard to find a course in the United States where any of this is discussed.

VIJAY: It is almost impossible to find any real discussion about the underlying issues of the political tussles that occur on the front pages of the newspapers and in the leading stories on television. For instance, there will be stories about the refugee crisis across the Mediterranean, there will be stories about the NATO–Russia standoff on the Ukraine border, and there will be stories about the negotiations in Vienna over the nuclear deal with Iran. But these are all interlinked stories. In short order, thanks to U.S.-imposed conflicts, Europe lost access to its three sources of energy: Iran, due to the sanctions regime put in place starting from 2006; Libya, due to NATO's war in 2011 that disrupted the entire oil infrastructure and the legal basis for ownership of the oil; and Russia, due to the conflict over Ukraine in 2014. Europe lost access to natural gas and oil. European self-interest seemed to be totally forgotten.

173

NOAM: The case of Libya was not predicted. They didn't expect to destroy Libya. Libya has sweet oil; it is very accessible, and it is close to Europe. Access to Libyan oil was surely a goal of the NATO intervention. It is one of those unfortunate things that goes wrong. In the case of Iran, Europe wants to get access to the Iranian market, but there a superior consideration arises, namely that there is no appetite to confront the United States. That has been an issue for Europe since World War II. There have been efforts in Europe to move toward more independence: Charles de Gaulle attempted it, and *Ostpolitik*— West Germany's olive branch to the East—was an effort in this direction. But they were always beaten back, and the European ruling class—the business world, the political elite—always decided finally to simply be subordinate to the United States and be part of the U.S. system. Gorbachev's idea to create a United Eurasia can never be in the cards, because of overwhelming U.S. power, which does not support the self-interest of the European ruling classes. Europe certainly has the capacity to develop its own financial system and challenge the U.S. domination of financial networks, but that's a very different kind of world. It would mean the world breaking up into different kinds of blocs, with the United States linked up with

Britain and other Atlantic powers (Canada, for example) and then with Europe linked up with Russia and China. The European ruling class has never wanted that since its business sector is tightly entangled with the United States to the point where they are almost indistinguishable.

It is a constant conflict within the European ruling class and within the ruling classes of different European countries and sectors. This is clear with Nord Stream 2. Large sections of the German ruling class want the pipeline from Russia. The United States wants to block it, and so do the parts of Europe that are dependent on the United States. The relationship between the United States, Europe, and energy goes back to the postwar period. The Marshall Plan, set in motion after World War II, was in large part a U.S. program to convert Europe from reliance upon coal to reliance upon oil. Coal was abundant in Europe, which had no oil. If they became oil based, the United States would have "veto power" (George Kennan's phrase, referring specifically to Japan) over Europe because the United States would control their energy supplies. Ten percent of the Marshall Plan money—about $1.2 billion—was shifted among U.S. banks as they converted Europe into an oil-based economy. This oil was not going to come from the United States, but from the Middle East; by 1950,

85 percent of Europe's oil needs were supplied from the Middle East, which the United States controlled and profited from. The same process was imposed on Japan. As Western Europe and Japan were converted to oil-based economies, the United States had veto power over them. Zbigniew Brzezinski said he was against the U.S. invasion of Iraq, but since it was going to happen, he felt it would allow the United States to control Iraqi oil and then gain more leverage over Europe. These kinds of thoughts have never been far from ruling-class considerations. Europe has consistently chosen to be a subordinate to the United States rather than strike out on its own; of course, Europe can be on its own, since it has a larger population than the United States, more wealth, and a more highly educated population. If Europe strikes out on its own, it will come as a radical reorientation of the world system.

5

Fragilities of U.S. Power

VIJAY: When Russia invaded Ukraine, the United States put pressure on Germany to ban the import of natural gas and to prevent the certification of the Nord Stream 2 pipeline. Germany's chancellor Olaf Scholz said that any such ban would plunge Germany into a terrible recession. Germany's initial waffling over the Nord Stream 2 pipeline has both commercial and geopolitical implications. The pipeline and its construction concerns firms from a range of countries, including Switzerland and China. The natural gas was going to come to Europe from fields that will now also supply China via the Power of Siberia 2 pipeline complex. This means that Russia will no longer rely upon the European market. Russia has tried to "sanctions-proof" its economy, reducing dollar reserves as part of its central bank reserves (increasing euros, gold, and renminbi) as well as cutting back on reliance upon Western ownership of Russian government bonds. This has, of course, made Russia less vulnerable to sanctions, to future external shocks, and to sudden sell-off. The key word here is "less." The sanctions placed after the Russian invasion of Ukraine have had an impact not only on Russia, but on the Central Asian states—which are integrated into the Russian economy—and, due to Ukraine and Russia being the major grain providers of the world, on the world food

179

system. The new arrangements set up by Russia before the war, such as the renminbi holdings and the attempt to create an alternative wire-transfer system to the Europe-based SWIFT network, follow the gradual tightening of relations between Russia and China, which were adversaries during the Cold War but are now close allies. The relationship is based on a common understanding of the need for multipolarity rather than a U.S.-dominated system, as well as on mutual trade and security benefits that have emerged over the past few decades. The increasing fragility of U.S. power comes at a time when China has emerged with self-confidence, its science and technology industries buoyant and its recovery from the COVID-19 crisis exemplary, for now. The U.S.-imposed hybrid war on China is part of a general frustration that Western firms have not been able to compete against the dynamism of Chinese firms, particularly in the hi-tech sectors. NATO has begun to assert a new brand identity, Global NATO. As part of this new brand, NATO has argued that its principal adversary is China. This is a conflict from which there is no withdrawal possible, because this is an existential conflict. NATO is in the midst of a dangerous confrontation with Russia and a serious escalation against China, building up bases around China and militarizing the Arctic Circle.

NOAM: Well, Russia and China were bitter enemies right through the 1960s. They were, in fact, at war with each other, with their long border heavily fortified. Over the past few decades, Russia and China have developed more cooperative relations. China is trying to integrate Central Asia, Africa, and, to the extent possible, Latin America into a China-based system. The Shanghai Cooperation Organization (SCO) has been the official framework for this development, and the Belt and Road Initiative (BRI) is the commercial axis. The SCO now includes all of the Central Asian states, along with Russia, India, Pakistan, Iran, possibly soon Afghanistan, aiming for Turkey and then Eastern and maybe Central Europe. The United States applied for observer status, not membership, and was rebuffed. The SCO is building a Eurasian network in the way Gorbachev had imagined it. If the Chinese can integrate the European powers into this network through the BRI and Nord Stream 2, if Russia and China can continue to cooperate, then in the long term you will get this kind of continental integration.

The Chinese have established a thousand vocational schools in Southeast Asia and Africa to train students in the new Chinese technologies. These are efficient technologies that will integrate these countries and their development into the China-based BRI system. The Chinese are sharing this technology in very poor parts of the world at prices that are reasonable for those economies. They have developed leading technologies in robotics, green energy, and telecommunications. It's a very personal issue, incidentally. Where I live, which is partly rural, there is very poor internet service. If we were allowed to bring Huawei technology, we'd have 5G internet. We badly need solar panels, and the most technologically advanced and cheapest ones are made in China.

Chinese leaders understand very well that their country's maritime trade routes are ringed with hostile powers, from Japan through the Malacca Straits and beyond, backed by overwhelming U.S. military force. Accordingly, China is proceeding to expand westward with extensive investments and careful moves toward integration. China is constructing a modernized version of the old silk roads, with the intent not only of integrating the region under Chinese influence, but also of reaching Europe and the Middle Eastern oil-producing regions. It is pouring huge sums into creating an integrated Asian energy and commercial system, with extensive high-speed rail lines and energy pipelines. One element of the program is a highway through some of the world's tallest mountains to the new Chinese-developed port of Gwadar in Pakistan, which will protect oil shipments from potential U.S. interference. The program might also, China and Pakistan hope, spur industrial development in Pakistan, which the United States has not undertaken despite massive military aid, and might also provide an incentive for Pakistan to clamp down on domestic terrorism, a serious issue for China in western Xinjiang province. Gwadar will be part of China's "string of pearls"—bases being constructed along the Indian Ocean for commercial purposes but potentially also for military use, with the expectation that China might someday be able to project power as far as the Persian Gulf for the first time in the modern era.

All of these moves remain immune to Washington's overwhelming military power, short of annihilation by nuclear war, which would destroy the United States as well. In 2015, China also established the Asian Infrastructure Investment Bank, with itself as the main shareholder. Fifty-six nations participated in the opening in Beijing in June 2015, including U.S. allies Australia, Britain, and others, which joined in defiance of Washington's wishes. The United States and Japan were absent. Some analysts believe that the new bank might turn out to be a competitor to the Bretton Woods institutions (the IMF and the World Bank), in which the United States holds veto power. There are also some expectations that the SCO might eventually become a counterpart to NATO.

If we return to the question of Afghanistan, there are two approaches to deal with the immense crisis there. The U.S. approach is to blockade the country. The other approach, from the SCO, is to try to integrate Afghanistan into the massive Eurasian system. They say, *The Taliban is the government. We have to deal with them. We will try to induce them to become more inclusive, maybe to moderate their behavior. Let's hope to shift the economy from producing heroin for the West to mining its rich mineral resources, which we in China will be happy to make use of. We will move in that direction and provide immediate aid to end the humanitarian crisis.*

The plan therefore is to stop China from developing. A lot of U.S. policy under Trump and then Biden has been to try to block the threat of Chinese development. They are continuing to try to ban Huawei technology on the grounds that there might be spyware in it; couldn't imagine that U.S.-based technology might be routinely infected with spyware (to spy on the correspondence of allies from Europe, as is occasionally uncovered). China refuses to surrender its technological developments. It cannot be intimidated, and it does not follow orders. It is like Cuba, but vastly more powerful. That's the real problem for the United States, and it could lead to war. If it leads to war, as you said, it would essentially be the end for everybody. The United States and China simply must cooperate if the world's going to survive.

The United States accuses China of being against the "rules-based order," but in fact remember that there are two competing conceptions of the world order on the table. The "rules-based order" is supported by the United States, which defines the system as, *If you follow the United States then you are following the rules.* The other system is the UN-based international order, which is grounded in the UN Charter and is advocated for and often followed by the Chinese.

VIJAY: The United States, which continues to increase its military spending, suggests that the Chinese are the threat to the world system. By the estimates at SIPRI, the United States spent at least $778 billion in 2020 on its military, while China spent $252 billion. Let's not even put this in per capita terms or deal with this spending historically, when the United States far outstrips Chinese spending on weaponry. Nonetheless, it is China that is positioned in the general Western discourse as a threat.

NOAM: In the *New York Times*, David Sanger and William Broad, two of its leading military correspondents, describe the concern of the U.S. military with the Chinese military buildup.[1] The Chinese are threatening U.S. missile defenses off the coast of China and are building a tiny fraction of the number of nuclear missiles that the United States has. There's something missing here in this coverage. It's not just U.S. missile defense systems. The east coast of China is ringed with U.S. bases with nuclear armed missiles aimed at China. What about that? Are the Chinese concerned about that? Would we be concerned if China had dozens of bases along the Pacific or Atlantic coasts, with nuclear missiles aimed at the United States? Would that bother us? Well, it wouldn't bother us, because we'd destroy the world to make sure it didn't happen. But this doesn't even get mentioned. All that is mentioned is that they're threatening our means of defense off the coast of China. There will be no letter to the editor about it, because it is taken for granted. We have a right to defend ourselves against China by aiming nuclear missiles at them. One U.S. nuclear submarine with Trident missiles can destroy almost two hundred cities anywhere in the world. That's one submarine. They are seen as old-fashioned. So, the United States has to build new and more advanced submarines and missile systems. Is that seen as a threat to anyone? No. *God, how could it be? We are godlike people. How can anyone feel threatened by us!*

The U.S. military is driving us toward destruction through nuclear war and the climate catastrophe. We are not satisfied with being able to destroy the planet many times over; now we have to take our military ambitions into space. Every U.S. administration increases military spending. None reduce it. It would take a fraction of the military spending to invest in crumbling infrastructure and to fulfill necessary social needs. But you can't touch the military spending. It is almost surreal. Take the case of the missiles. Every strategic analyst knows that land-based missiles are more of a threat to the country that has them than to the adversary. The United States has about a thousand land-based missiles. They're all targeted. Any adversary knows exactly where they are down to a couple of kilometers. If a threat develops, the adversary can destroy these missiles. The U.S. command knows this and calls them "use them or lose them" missiles. You either fire them off immediately or you lose them. This means that if there is tension anywhere in the world, you have the necessity to fire them. Using them means that you are destroyed by a retaliatory strike. They are now upgrading the land-based missile system. It would be a great advantage for American security if they were simply destroyed. And they don't even have to be reciprocal. If the Russians want to harm themselves, okay. Let them do it by having land-based missiles. Even unilateral destruction of them would be advantageous. But instead they're being upgraded. The Pentagon has been clever. They distribute these land-based missiles around rural areas, in many parts of the country where the local congressman is going to ensure that they stay there. Because they bring a couple of jobs to the local community. And especially with the neoliberal globalization and its destruction of rural America, that's what they hang on to. So, there are local forces, which say, *Let's endanger ourselves as much as possible.* And you can't touch the military, just like you can't touch the fossil fuel companies or the banks. You know? These are institutional failures, which are extremely deep, and they simply must be overcome quickly, or we're just finished. Can't survive this dysfunctional society. Impossible.

VIJAY: Our world has truly entered a dysfunctional phase. The Russian military intervention of Ukraine in February 2022 set the dial closer to annihilation. There was even loose talk about nuclear war. Of course, this war, like other wars before it is horrendous. The international division of humanity has made its appearance once more, with talk of blue eyes and blonde hair making this a conflict to consider, whereas the brutality inflicted upon Iraq and on Yemen is set aside.

NOAM: Don't forget Afghanistan. Millions face imminent starvation, the U.S. robs Afghan funds, people with bank accounts cannot access them to buy food. This is maybe the cruelest of current crimes, after twenty years of battering the country to dust.

VIJAY: A fair question could be asked whether this war has the potential to change the world order or is it merely accelerating changes that were already in motion?

Of the many outcomes of this war, two stare us in the face. The first is that the United States is going to be able to revive Europe's subordinated status. All talk of "Gaulism" on the continental scale through Europe's Common Foreign and Security Policy (CFSP) seems to be

189

now set aside as NATO—with the United States in the driver's seat—dictating policy. There was an attempt to create an independent European foreign policy through the Maastricht Treaty (1993) and the Amsterdam Treaty (1997). But these were crushed by the U.S.-driven NATO war on Yugoslavia (1999), which held German ambitions in check and yoked European policy to that of its NATO headquarters and, farther afield, to the United States. NATO's war in Afghanistan (2001–2021) and Libya (2011) strengthened the U.S. control over European foreign policy. After the Lisbon Treaty (2007), the EU created a High Representative on CFSP, a role that remains relatively unimportant (except in the negotiation with Iran, where the EU mostly advanced U.S. arguments). During this Russian war in Ukraine, European foreign policy will not be able to develop independently but will remain captive to that of the United States. The price—higher food and energy costs—will be paid by the European people.

NOAM: Before you get to the second point, it is important to point out that NATO's war on Yugoslavia in 1999 might be the real turning point for Russia with Europe in thrall to the United States as it pursued an unprovoked aggression, an aggression covered up with incredible lying, which persists to the present.

VIJAY: The second is that the institutional and trade linkages created by China—in particular—but also Russia will accelerate. This will be first and foremost between China and Russia, whose closeness has developed over the past decade. But it will open outward in arenas not previously recognized, such as with the growth of a greater pressure in the Global South toward multipolarity and nonalignment. You already saw that in the first UN General Assembly vote on the Russian war, where the Global South largely abstained from condemnation. Then countries such as India—otherwise close to the United States—refusing to break ties with Russia. Other interesting developments have been taking place here, as the contradictions open up: pressure on the U.S. to lighten sanctions against Iran and Venezuela for the sake of bringing energy prices down, and new ties between the United Arab Emirates and Syria, as the Gulf countries firm up their linkages with both China and Russia. So, while Europe chose to take cover under the security umbrella of the United States, the rest of the world seems to understand this new situation as potentially accelerating a new phase of nonalignment and multipolarity.

NOAM: Yes. Russia will likely drift further into China's orbit, becoming even more of a declining kleptocratic raw materials producer than it is now. China is likely to persist in its programs of incorporating more and more of the world into the development-and-investment system based on the Belt and Road Initiative, the "maritime silk road" that passes through the UAE into the Middle East, and the Shanghai Cooperation Organization. The U.S. seems intent on responding with its comparative advantage: force. Right now, that includes Biden's programs of "encirclement" of China by military bases and alliances, while perhaps even seeking to improve the U.S. economy as long as it is framed as competing with China. Just what we are observing now.

The most significant effect of this war, barely discussed, is that it sets back—maybe permanently—the meager hopes for escaping the total catastrophe of climate destruction, the end of organized human life (and innumerable other species we are wantonly destroying). During the war, the UN Framework Convention on Climate Change released an interim report that showed the governments of the world nowhere near making any commitment to limit climate change to 1.5°C and meet the goals of the Paris Agreement. The UN Secretary-General António Guterres said that this was a "red alert for our planet." No such alarm was on the front pages of the newspapers. The glee in the executive offices of the fossil fuel companies, now free to accelerate total destruction, perhaps even exceeds the glee in the offices of military contractors.

The game is not over. There is still time for radical course correction. The means are understood. If the will is there, it is possible to avert catastrophe and to move on to a much better world.

Afterword

Thirty Years of Writing and Speaking with Noam Chomsky

BY VIJAY PRASHAD

Not long ago, I went through some old boxes and found letters that I had exchanged with Noam Chomsky from the first years of the 1990s. I had written to him after a brief meeting at his office at MIT (Cambridge, Massachusetts, United States), where Noam opened his doors to anyone who wanted to talk. A deeply democratic man in every aspect, Noam inquired about my background and told me about his connection to linguistics professors in the city of my birth, Calcutta, India. We discussed the work I was then doing on a Dalit community in northern India and the contradictory pressures on Dalit workers as a consequence of the opening up or liberalization of the Indian economy in 1991. Later, when I wrote to him about an essay I had written about these themes, he wished me luck with its publication and asked me to send him a finished copy. When I did, he wrote back with his thoughts about the essay, clearly having read it carefully and having thought about the points I had made about informal migrant labor and the political implications of what I had found during my interviews with workers in and around Delhi. I could not believe that Noam Chomsky—yes, *the* Noam Chomsky—had taken so much interest in my work and that he had advised me despite the fact that we had no formal institutional connection.

Each of the typed letters carries his personal stories of his time in this or that part of the world. In 1996, I sent him an article I had written on the Emergency (1975–1977) in India, which he said he read "with more than the usual interest since I'd just returned from India, where I had managed to spend a day in the countryside outside Calcutta, visiting self-governing villages, accompanied by an agricultural-economist friend (V. K. Ramachandran) who works in West Bengal and Kerala mainly, and the Minister of Finance (who turns out to be an MIT economic graduate)." This was when the Left Front formed the government in West Bengal, the finance minister being Asim Dasgupta. "It was very fascinating and impressive, and I heard a fair amount about the brutal repression of the '70s there, which I'd known virtually nothing about. Apparently, these struggles were a significant factor in carrying out what seems to

be one of the rare implementations in India of the panchay-
at [local self-government] provisions of the constitution,"
wrote Noam. In the article I had sent him, which was later
published in *Social Scientist* (1996), Noam noticed that I
had been reading about slum clearance in Delhi. "I saw a
piece of this by chance when I was in India in 1972," he
wrote, "giving a Nehru memorial lecture and a number of
others in Delhi. There was a big squatter settlement there,
downtown. One day, on the way from the hotel to a talk
somewhere, we drove past, and it was gone. Vanished. I
asked what had happened and was told that it was cleared
out, the people dumped somewhere in the countryside many
miles away, because an Asian fair was going to open, and it
wouldn't look good. That was during the period of democracy!" In the early 1990s, I had done part of my dissertation
research in the resettlement colonies that had been in the
countryside, and which had become a key part of Delhi.
It was these areas that were the epicenter of anti-Muslim
violence in 1993 (which I directly witnessed) and again in
2020.

In 1996, when I went to Turkey for a brief trip to cover
the renewed violence in the southeast, I sent Noam a few
letters with clippings from my stories that had been published in *Frontline*. Noam knew *Frontline* well since he had

been interviewed by and put on the cover of the magazine on several occasions (including an interview with me). This time we exchanged thoughts on Turkey, only fragments of that conversation remaining in the letters that I have from Noam. But I recall them well, since he not only told me to be careful in a difficult context, but also offered me a contextual assessment of the Turkish state's relationship with the Kurdish people and of the great complexity of Turkish nationalism, a national project that emerged as the Ottoman Empire collapsed in 1922 and as the new republican Turkey came to terms—including through genocidal violence—with questions of ethnicity and of citizenship. Two points are important to underscore: the care Noam showed for my safety (which touched me greatly) and the importance of Noam's contextualization for the deadline journalism that I was then producing. From his first political book (*American Power and the New Mandarins*), Noam has understood U.S. power not in the minutiae of its reproduction but through a long-term perspective that seeks to understand its generative grammar, to steal from Noam's linguistics. This habit of contextualization, of setting current events in terms of their historical dynamics and in terms of the sociology of power, is Noam's greatest contribution to our understanding of our times. In other words, unlike scores of scholars of international relations, Noam did not insist on this or that model as the basis of understanding events and processes; rather, he had a method (rooted in history and the sociology of power) he used in a supple way to generate a theory of our times. Even when we do not agree about this or that assessment, it is this Chomsky model for understanding the present that shaped the way I reported stories as a journalist from Peru to Afghanistan.

Many intellectuals develop a deeply critical stance about this or that aspect of reality—critical, for instance, of the way governments collude with energy corporations to destroy the planet, or of the way this or that government behaves toward its people. But there are few intellectuals—Noam at the head—who have held fast to a position against the most powerful entities in the world, organized and led by the United States' ruling class. Coterminous with the U.S. escalation of its war in Indochina, Noam developed a fine-grained understanding of the structural causes of the Godfather attitude of the U.S. ruling class. Not once in the decades since then has Noam shied away from his fundamental disdain for the violent use of power by the ruling class of the United States. This disdain has been shaped by close encounters with the survivors of that power, whether in the Plain of Jars (Laos, 1970) or the Gaza Strip (Palestine,

2012). Each of these visits strengthened Noam's views of the world and deepened his commitment to those courageous people, as he puts it at the start of this book; Noam's theory of the world is not developed in the MIT library alone, but elaborated in his visits to places such as Diyarbakir (Turkey) and Caracas (Venezuela), where he accompanied those who saw U.S. imperialism from the standpoint of its victims. There is good reason why Noam's work is read so closely in places far from the United States, and why Venezuela's president Hugo Chávez held up Chomsky's *Hegemony and Survival: America's Quest for Global Dominance* (2003) at the United Nations General Assembly in 2006.

Noam's readers marvel at his learning and his ability to synthesize vast amounts of material, including the latest academic studies, publicly available government documents, and information that he has gleaned from social and political movements on the ground. After I reported a story for *Frontline* in 1999 on the current situation in Colombia, Noam wrote, "I was particularly interested in the documentation that Ricardo gave FARC on the regime's links with paras and narco-traffickers. Is that public? Available? I hadn't been aware of it." Noam is referring to Victor Ricardo, who was the peace commissioner for the Colombian government at this time, and whose documents I had been able to read in Bogotá that year. Having read such documents carefully, sent to him by activists and journalists such as myself, Noam was able to build his powerful critique of Plan Colombia, the U.S. government policy to finance and arm the Colombian government—knee deep in complicity with the paramilitaries and with the narco-traffickers—against any and all dissent (this assessment appeared in Noam's *Rogue States*, 2000). No wonder that Eduardo Galeano referred to the Colombian "democracy" as *democradura* or a "democratatorship" (as Noam noted in his introduction to Javier Giraldo's *Colombia: The Genocidal Democracy*, 1996). Noam's is not the view from Washington, but a view *of* Washington built through research of what occurs at the peripheries. Washington is attacked by Noam not for its internal schisms, but for the implications of its policy—Plan Colombia, in this case—against ordinary people far away— the peasantry of Colombia, in this case; it is information about and from those peasants that informs the *stance* of Noam Chomsky.

For a variety of reasons, Noam has a reputation for cold-blooded analysis. Part of that comes from his forensic use of information and his insistence that conveying information in as dry a manner as possible is sufficient to awaken insight in his audiences. Noam does not bang his podium or stamp his feet; he remains at the level of facts, facts being the sharpened sword in his intellectual arsenal. But these are not merely facts; they are facts that he has unearthed because he has been taught to read and to look for facts in places that people do not know exist, and because he is able to marshal these facts into a theory of the world that is otherwise little known because of the fog of manufactured consent. If you listen carefully to Noam Chomsky, however, you will hear someone with an immense sense of humor—*imagine if a journalist from Mars arrived at Columbia*—and you might detect his outrage at the way things are done in our world. "Lunatics," he writes to me during the NATO war on Yugoslavia. No other way to describe the protagonists of Washington's war, which accelerated the killings on the ground in Kosovo. That sense of outrage is evident in the conversations that shape this book, where he—even in his factual style—breaks free and talks with great feeling about the atrocities visited upon the Afghans, the Iraqis, the Libyans, and others. I hope that readers understand that Noam's immense example is built from his giving close attention to the voices of victims of imperialism and his fidelity to their humanity and their struggles.

Visiting Chomsky in Building 20 at MIT was always a treat, not only because of the conversations with Noam but also because of the building itself. Built as a temporary structure during World War II, Building 20 housed MIT's linguistics faculty until it was demolished in 1998 and replaced by the Strata Center. There was something wonderful about the building, since it was such a simple, unpretentious structure on a campus devoted to the most sophisticated technology. The building reflected the attitude of Noam himself, a distinguished linguist whose breakthroughs refashioned his own field. It is hard to read his writings on linguistics, which are technical and require training to decipher. But Noam does not bring this atmosphere to his writings on the world, which are deeply democratic in their style and form. While the academy encourages specialization and opacity of language due to the narrowness of the various specialties, Noam sets that aside once he leaves the field of linguistics and provides a model for democratic communication, offering his vast knowledge and wisdom in the service of movements for social transformation. Of course, Noam will say—and he is right—that he is not the only person like this, but of course that does not minimize what he provides.

In 1988, journalist Glenn Frankel reviewed Edward Said and Christopher Hitchens's *Blaming the Victim* in the *Washington Post*. Noam has an essay in that book. Frankel called Noam's essay "breathlessly deranged." "I kind of like that," Noam says. "I think [Frankel] was wrong about the 'breathless'—if you read the article, it was pretty calm—but 'deranged' is correct. I mean, you have to be deranged to accept elementary moral truisms and to describe facts that shouldn't be described. That's probably true" (*Media Control*, 2002). Here, you get the sense of humor, the adherence to unpopular facts, and the stance for a moral position against injustice and for equality. That's Noam in a nutshell.

Noam sharpened his pencil on the lies of the U.S. government and the hopes of the ordinary people of the world.

I first encountered Noam through his book *American Power and the New Mandarins* (1969), tucked away on my parents' bookshelf in Calcutta. The book was given to my father in 1969 by my aunt, Brinda Karat, now a leader of the Communist Party of India (Marxist). There is a funny story about the book. My aunt, who worked for Air India at that time and had led a protest that changed the airline's dress code, and my brother went to one of the many protests in London against the U.S. war on Vietnam. My father arrived there and was angry that my brother had been taken to the protests. My father and aunt argued. She took her copy of Chomsky's book, cut out her name from the title page, and dedicated it to my father with love and affection. My father carried that book back from London. I found that book years later, prominently shelved next to some of his favorite books. I read it as I read everything on that bookshelf (such as books by Anthony Sampson, including *The Money Lenders* and *Seven Sisters*). I remember puzzling over the dedication to *American Power*: "To the brave young men who refused to serve in a criminal war." Calcutta was an unusual place. The street that housed the U.S. and British consulates had been renamed Ho Chi Minh Sarani, and demonstrations were a regular feature there through the early 1970s. Chomsky's book was in solidarity with the Vietnamese, whom he had met during his visit to North Vietnam in 1970, with the U.S. youth who refused to fight and who formed a detachment in the antiwar struggle, and with those who stood at places such as Chowringhee, at the mouth of Ho Chi Minh Sarani, chanting slogans against the war: *tomar nam, amar nam, Vietnam, Vietnam* (Your name, my name: Vietnam, Vietnam). It has been a long journey for me, to read Noam on intellectuals who dance between the lure of complicity and the courage of commitment, to read Noam on U.S. imperialism, to read Noam on the Middle East, to read Noam on Central America, to read Noam on East Timor, to read Noam on Yugoslavia. I learned my geography and ethics from Noam. That learning continued during the conversation that produced *The Withdrawal*.

Notes

9/11 and Afghanistan

1. Rodric Braithwaite, "New Afghan Myths Bode Ill for Western aims," *Financial Times*, October 15, 2008.

2. Noam Chomsky, "What Americans Have Learnt—and Not Learnt—Since 9/11," *The Age*, September 7, 2002.

3. Samuel Huntington, "The Lonely Superpower," *Foreign Affairs*, March/April 1999.

4. "Confiscating Solar Panels from Palestinians in August Is Abuse," *Haaretz*, August 22, 2021.

5. Armando Chaguaceda and Coco Fusco, "Cubans Want Much More than an End to the U.S. Embargo," *New York Times*, August 7, 2021.

6. Russell Baker, "A Heroic Historian on Heroes," *New York Review of Books*, June 11, 2009.

Iraq

1. Knut Royce, "Secret Offer: Iraq Sent Pullout Deal to U.S.," *Newsday*, August 29, 1990.

2. Patrick Tyler, "Confrontation in the Gulf: Arafat Eases Stand on Kuwait–Palestine Link," *New York Times*, January 3, 1991.

3. Thomas Friedman, "Vote France Off the Island," *New York Times*, February 9, 2003.

4. Richard A. Oppel Jr., "Early Target of Offensive Is a Hospital," *New York Times*, November 8, 2004.

5. "Iraq War Illegal, Says Annan," BBC, September 16, 2004.

6. "One Way Forward on Iran: A Nuclear-Weapons-Free Persian Gulf," *New York Times*, June 12, 2021.

Libya

1. Joshua Itzkowitz Shifrinson, "Deal or No Deal? The End of the Cold War and the U.S. Offer to Limit NATO Expansion," *International Security* 40, no. 4 (Spring 2016).

2. Ian Urbina, "The Secretive Prisons that Keep Migrants Out of Europe," *New Yorker*, November 28, 2021.

Fragilities of U.S. Power

1. David Sanger and William Broad, "As China Speeds Up Nuclear Arms Race, the U.S. Wants to Talk," *New York Times*, November 28, 2021.

About the Authors

Noam Chomsky is Institute Professor (emeritus) in the Department of Linguistics and Philosophy at the Massachusetts Institute of Technology and Laureate Professor of Linguistics and Agnese Nelms Haury Chair in the Program in Environment and Social Justice at the University of Arizona. A world-renowned linguist and political activist, he is the author of numerous books, including *On Language, Understanding Power* (edited by Peter R. Mitchell and John Schoeffel), *American Power and the New Mandarins, For Reasons of State, Problems of Knowledge and Freedom, Objectivity and Liberal Scholarship, Towards a New Cold War, The Essential Chomsky* (edited by Anthony Arnove), *On Anarchism, The Chomsky–Foucault Debate* (with Michel Foucault). He lives in Tucson, Arizona.

Vijay Prashad is director of Tricontinental: Institute for Social Research, editor of LeftWord Books, and chief correspondent for Globetrotter Independent Media Institute. He is the author of *Uncle Swami: South Asians in America Today* and *The Darker Nations: A People's History of the Third World*, as well as *The Karma of Brown Folk*. *The Darker Nations* won the Muzaffar Ahmad Book Prize. He lives in Santiago, Chile.

Publishing in the Public Interest

Thank you for reading this book published by The New Press. The New Press is a nonprofit, public interest publisher. New Press books and authors play a crucial role in sparking conversations about the key political and social issues of our day.

We hope you enjoyed this book and that you will stay in touch with The New Press. Here are a few ways to stay up to date with our books, events, and the issues we cover:

- Sign up at www.thenewpress.com/subscribe to receive updates on New Press authors and issues and to be notified about local events
- Like us on Facebook: www.facebook.com/newpressbooks
- Follow us on Twitter: www.twitter.com/thenewpress
- Follow us on Instagram: www.instagram.com/thenewpress

Please consider buying New Press books for yourself; for friends and family; or to donate to schools, libraries, community centers, prison libraries, and other organizations involved with the issues our authors write about.

The New Press is a 501(c)(3) nonprofit organization. You can also support our work with a tax-deductible gift by visiting www.thenewpress.com/donate.